A Conscious Person's Guide to the Workplace

Order this book online at www.trafford.com
or email orders@trafford.com

Most Trafford titles are also available at major online book retailers.

© Copyright 2010, 2011 George SanFacon.
Book and cover design by hEDWERXdESIGN
www.hedwerxdesign.com

Note for Librarians: A cataloguing record for this book is available from Library
and Archives Canada at www.collectionscanada.ca/amicus/index-e.html

Printed in the United States of America.

ISBN: 978-1-4251-6680-9 (sc)
ISBN: 978-1-4251-7467-5 (hc)

Trafford rev. 05/27/2011

 www.trafford.com

North America & international
toll-free: 1 888 232 4444 (USA & Canada)
phone: 250 383 6864 ♦ fax: 812 355 4082

A CONSCIOUS PERSON'S GUIDE TO THE WORKPLACE

GEORGE SANFACON

To Alex and Michael…
May you live in a world
that works for all.

DEDICATION

TABLE OF CONTENTS

Try to love the questions themselves…
The point is to live everything. Live the questions now.
Perhaps you will then gradually, without noticing it,
live your way some distant day into the answers.

~Ranier Maria Rilke

AUTHOR'S NOTE

Greetings.

This is my attempt to write the primer on *work, organizations,* and *management* that I was always looking for but never found. It is based on four decades of workplace experience, going back to my first job bagging groceries early in high school. By the time I graduated, I was working full-time on second shift in a factory. Since then, I have worked as a painter, mechanic, custodian, security guard, high school teacher, short-order cook, facilities engineer, energy conservation consultant, trainer, facilitator, operations manager, management consultant, and executive coach. In those capacities I have worked in grocery stores, factories, schools, libraries, apartment buildings, bowling alleys, conference and retreat centers, private homes, restaurants, colleges, and on delivery trucks. When I first wrote this, I was working as a director in facilities and operations management at a public university.

Almost without exception, regardless where I have worked or what my job was, I found the workplace experience to be lacking. So did my family and friends. The fact is, the vast majority of our workplaces do not meet the needs of the people working there. Even worse, many of them are killing grounds of the human spirit. Ironically, this undermines what our organizations are trying to accomplish in the first place. The resulting losses to ourselves, our organizations, and our society are enormous. The situation is one of the great tragedies of modern life and part of the unfinished business of our society. For several years now, I have been reading, reflecting, and working on this issue.

As a teenager I believed that I would eventually know the answers to life's most important questions. Actually, I thought I would have things pretty much figured out by the time I was thirty. But over the years (sixty now, to be exact) I came to understand that life's journey is not so much a matter of finding the right answers as living with the right questions—questions that matter—such as: What are human beings?…What is the purpose of work?…What is the nature of legitimate power and leadership?…What kind of workplaces and world do we want to create for ourselves and the generations that follow?… And what, if anything, is ultimately important?

Living with these kinds of questions can help us to "wake up" from the trance of conventional CULTure, gradually living our way into alternatives and answers. What follows are the ones that I've lived into along my journey. I share them with hope that they will help you to live your way into the answers that are right for you and for those affected by you. May they serve you well. And may they help promote a world that works for all.

George

Sunnyside
Brooklyn, Michigan
November 2007

Mind is the master weaver,
both of the inner garment of character
and the outer garment of circumstance.

~James Allen

INTRODUCTION

This guide is about creating alternatives to what we normally experience at work, ones that better promote human well being and engage the spirit. We can attempt to create such alternatives by layering new approaches and systems on the surface of the old, or by embracing different ways of thinking that give rise to the kind of experiences and workplaces for which we are yearning. What follows is about doing the latter: it outlines a different and unconventional way of thinking about the nature of work and workplaces. As systems thinker Peter Senge put it:

> The most radical aspect of the way we approach things
> is to focus on thinking. Most people believe you change
> organizations by rearranging external conditions: the
> reward systems, the information technologies. Our premise
> is that organizations are the way they are because of how
> people think. Until we change how we think...nothing
> really changes.[1]

In most workplaces, things like quality, productivity, and profit are thought of and pursued as primary outcomes and results. People, on the other hand, are thought of and treated as means to those ends—"human resources" used to achieve desired outcomes. The following is based on a different way of thinking—"that work exists for the person as much as the person exists for work...that the [enterprise] exists as much to provide meaningful work to the person as it exists to provide a product and service to the customer."[2] From this perspective, work is a vehicle of growth, enjoyment, and service for us. As such, it can unleash the power of the human spirit, encompassing the intangibles of morale, commitment, joy, energy, and love. When it does, the natural by-products include higher levels of productivity, creativity, and quality. This is because the human spirit is naturally generous; "the instant we are filled, our first impulse is to be useful, to be kind, to give something away."[3]

A surprisingly different array of notions about work and workplaces can be discovered (or rediscovered) through a more balanced and wholistic approach. For example: Work is not only about making a living and producing things, it is also about making a life and completing ourselves as human beings...Organizations are not simply enterprises that produce goods and services, but also forms of human community that further a satisfying and meaningful life experience... Legitimate leadership is not about privilege and the exercise of power, but about service and the empowerment of others...Creating better workplaces is no different than creating better selves and a better world.

What follows is both a personal statement of mine and a compendium of the wisdom of others. As such, it is a "commons" book — drawn, condensed, and integrated from hundreds of sources and a wide range of disciplines encompassing the fields of anthropology, biological science, business management, cosmology, organizational development, psychology, quantum physics, sociology, the study of human consciousness, and various schools of spiritual practice. The latter, referred to herein as "the Wisdom Traditions," includes a common core of wisdom and insights about life and reality that has been taught by sages throughout history and across cultures. My intention in pulling this together was twofold: to create a general resource and guide for the workplace that serves all of us — from front line employees to boardroom executives — and to meaningfully connect our work and organizations with both our personal lives and a better world.

Unlike most books on work and management, this one starts at the beginning: the first chapter is on *people*. The following chapters address *work, service, organizations, governance, management, leaders* and *leadership*. The last chapter is on *change* and *transformation*. The chapters are each intended and written for study and use as both independant essays and as part of an integrated whole. Taken together, they can serve as a conceptual framework and common ground for creating and managing organizations and workplaces where people are moving toward the fullest participation in life—co-creating the kind of experiences and world that are right, good, and desirable. The concepts and principles have been field tested and proven to work, in some cases over millennia. More recently, my colleagues and I successfully used them over a decade and a half to create a system of shared governance to manage a large service enterprise. Both the department and the governance system were nationally recognized for their innovation and effectiveness.[4]

Most likely, you will discover that you already know much of what is written herein and, hopefully, you will find the material easy to read and understand. Nonetheless, for maximum benefit, it is best read and digested slowly in small bites. Using the material to transform a workplace is relatively simple but immensely challenging: *Hold the concepts and principles as compass and guide, then deal openly and forthrightly with whatever circumstances arise.* Checklists are provided to support that process.

We share…
a small planet traveling through space
during a relatively short flash of consciousness
between the miracle of birth
and the mystery of death.

~J. Samuel Bois

We each want
to love and be loved,
to belong,
to participate in community,
to have a sense of self-worth,
to have the opportunity to learn and grow
intellectually and spiritually,
and to find meaning, dignity, and peace.

~ Kent Keith

PEOPLE

W ork and organizations begin with people. But what *are* people? And what do we want for ourselves and others? Without some shared understanding about such questions, it is probably futile to think or write about work and workplaces. But such questions have been debated throughout history and given rise to conflicting answers, philosophies, and even religions.

WHAT ARE PEOPLE?

Consider the following range of answers to the simple question, What is a human being?

- a fleeting aggregate of atoms[5]

- a bipedal, carbon-based life form[6]

- a primate having an erect stance, an opposable thumb, the ability to make and use specialized tools, articulate speech, and a highly developed brain with the faculty of abstract thought[7]

- a thinking, feeling, self-moving, electrochemical organism in continuous transaction within a space-time environment[8]

- a river of energy and information that is constantly renewing itself[9]

- a being made by and in the image of God, and endowed with an immaterial, immortal soul that survives the body

- a spiritual being of light temporarily incarnate in a physical body[10]

- the consciousness…out of which all sentient and insentient beings are born, through which they move, and back into which they must return.[11]

Thus do we differ in answering one of the most basic questions we can ask about the nature of our existence. And who is to say who is right? But if the workplace is going to work for all of us, then we need concepts and frameworks that can embrace and hold all of these answers as possibilities.

Organizational jargon refers to people as "human resources" or "our most important assets," but consider the following definitions from a standard dictionary (emphasis added).

resource: some*thing* that lies ready for use... available *property*...a *means* of accomplishing something[12]

asset: any*thing* owned that has exchange... value...a valuable *thing*[13]

These terms reduce people to one of the inputs needed to achieve outputs. They thereby fail to encompass all of what we are as human beings, and worse, they unconsciously promote workplace cultures that are people-*using* rather than people-*building*. Because people intuitively know that they are more than mere instruments for achieving organizational outcomes, they often withhold parts of themselves and their potential contributions when treated as such.

Our Common Nature & Predicament

While it may not be possible to agree on *what* we are, we can probably agree on fundamental aspects of our common nature and predicament. With that in mind, the following is some of what we all share in being human.

We are...Unique Paradoxically, you are unique just like everyone else—a distinct, singular pulse in the cosmos. As editor and writer George Leonard so eloquently noted:

The ineluctable uniqueness of each individual...expresses itself in fingerprint, voiceprint, signature, scent, breathing pattern, brainwave, and, indeed, in every way of moving, every aspect of being.[14]

Native American culture holds that this uniqueness endows each of us with "original medicine." They encourage and nourish this uniqueness, considering it much needed by the community and found no where else on the planet.[15]

We are...Related To be human is to be related. Genetic scientists have concluded that every human being on the planet can trace his or her ancestry back to a single female living in North Africa approximately 150,000 years ago.[16] So we are all descendants of this African "Eve" and members of a single human family. And we are in this together; we came into existence through our parents, and required human relationships and support to mature and grow.

Besides this kinship and interdependency, we also share being part of the vast web of relationships that constitutes life on our planet. As civil rights leader Martin Luther King proclaimed: "All people of this world are tied into a single garment of destiny. Whatever affects one directly, affects all indirectly."[17] For thousands of years, mystics, seers, sages, and philosophers around the world have claimed that we are each connected to one another and to the totality of existence. More recently, leading scientists in fields as various as biology, cosmology, quantum physics, and consciousness are converging on the conclusion that:

> The...universe is a subtle but constant interconnection, a world where everything informs—acts on and interacts with—everything else...a universe where nothing disappears without a trace, and where all things that exist are, and remain, intrinsically and intimately interconnected"[18]

We are...Wholistic The various aspects of ourselves, including body, mind, and spirit, function as an integrated whole. "You can't hire a hand...You hire the whole person—feelings, human needs, social behavior, and...spirit."[19] We can see and experience this wholeness in our psychology and physiology, where there is a constant interaction between our thoughts, feelings, energy levels, spirit, and actions. This wholeness is also part of our evolutionary history and social heritage. Over the millennia, we evolved in small tribal bands where people participated in almost every aspect of their society. Daily activities were not isolated into separate fields such as *work*, *play*, and *education*, but were interwoven together as a whole with the rest of the life experience. And with the exception of part-time shamans, there were no social classes or specialized occupations that socially fragmented the tribe.[20] Our quest to find meaning and purpose in life further marks this wholistic nature, for the meaning of something is derived from its relationship to the greater whole. According to the dictionary, wholeness not only means "complete" but also means "not wounded...having been restored... [and] healed."[21] So the word *wholeness* is synonymous with *healing*. And much of the healing that we do relates to restoring wholeness in ourselves and society, as symbolized by the Medicine Wheel of the indigenous spiritual traditions.

We are...Emergent Psychologists generally agree that human development proceeds through three major stages: preconventional (selfish), conventional (caring) and postconventional (universal caring). Professor of psychiatry and writer Roger Walsh describes the first stages of that process as follows:

> We are born bewildered and unsocialized...with no coherent sense of ourselves as people and with no sense of the conventions of society. We are then gradually enculturated, informally by family and media, formally by the educational system....In this way we are introduced to—the conventional view of things. For the most part, we come to see and act as society suggests. We tend to assume that our culture's beliefs are valid...We also accept its worldview—its picture of the universe and ourselves.[22]

With even further development, we can gain some distance from our society, along with the capacity to criticize and reform it. This is the *postconventional* stage of development. But society does little to support our development to or at that level. Social systems and institutions are intended to conserve and preserve our way of living, not change it. Thus, every society has a cultural "center of gravity" that acts like a magnet on individual development.[23] And while this center tends to pull us up from infancy to conventionality, it also tends to hold us back from growing beyond there. If conventionality was Utopian, this would be okay, but it is associated with unfulfilling ways of living:

> [The] views from East and West, from religion, philosophy, and psychology all converge on a startling conclusion of enormous importance: *We are only half-grown and half-awake*...We live in the biggest cult of all, namely culture. Much of the misery in our lives, the turmoil in our relationships, and the tragedies in the world begin to make sense once these facts are appreciated. [24]

For the most part, *convention* is the story of one self or group of selves trying to dominate or subjugate another self or group of selves.[25] It is the story of scarcity and fear—the law of the jungle and survival of the fittest. But we can develop beyond convention. Interestingly, those who do so live far more satisfying lives than the rest of us: they feel better about themselves, revere life and nature, place less emphasis on social status and material possessions, and are more able to accept and embrace others. At the post conventional level, life becomes less of a *struggle* and more of a *dance*. And the many ways that we separate ourselves from each other are transcended: we are no longer concerned solely about ourselves, or our tribe, or our nation, but about "what is fair and right and just" for everyone, regardless of race, color, creed, or gender.[26] So we are unfinished, or *works in progress*, and one of the central purposes of our activities is to bring forth the latent possibilities that we each possess.

We are...Mortal Our bodies are open systems that burn bright but eventually go out. While we tend not think about it, we know there are physical limits to our time here and that sooner or later we will die.

> Today, approximately 200,000 people died. Some died by accident. Others by murder. Some by overeating. Others

from starvation. Some died while still in the womb. Others of old age. Some died of thirst. Others of drowning. Each died their death as they must. Some died in surrender, with their minds open and their hearts at peace. Others died in confusion, suffering from a life unlived.[27]

| THE BUDDHA'S TEACHER

The Buddha was widely recognized as someone who had studied and practiced many years to reach an enlightened state of being. People were, therefore, naturally curious about his teachers. It is said that when someone asked the Buddha if he had a special teacher, one that clearly stood out among the rest, he said, "Yes, of course." When pressed to identify who this great teacher was, he replied "Death."

Job titles, social position, material possessions, sexual roles and images—all must yield to death…In consciously honoring the fact of our physical death, we are thereby empowered to penetrate the social pretense, ostentation, and confusion that normally obscure our sense of what is truly significant. An awareness of death is an ally for infusing our lives with a sense of immediacy, perspective, and proportion. In acknowledging the reality of death, we can fully appreciate our gift of life.[28]

Because death is certain and inevitable, life itself, including each member of the human family, is inconceivably precious.

We are…Self-Aware We are self-reflective beings, consciously aware of our functioning, relationships, and mortality. We are also aware of our awareness: not only do we participate in the life experience, but we can also observe that experience and observe our observing. Seeker and spiritual teacher Ram Dass refers to this capacity in the following:

[What] do I see when I look at another human being?...I see body...Tune a little deeper, there's personality. Now tune once more, and here we are...It's like you're sitting inside that package and I'm sitting inside this package."[29]

This self-awareness gives rise to our sense of conscience and free will, and to the big questions that we live with: What is going on?...Who am I?...Who or what created the universe?...How am I related to the Creator or the Creative Principle?...What is the purpose of my life, or life in general?[30] Each of us has our own answers, and these can change at different stages of our lives. Nevertheless, the capacity to ask such questions means that there are two realms of our reality — the realm of *form* and the realm of *consciousness*, the exterior that can be seen by others and the interior that only we can know.

> The first is the everyday realm with which we are all
> familiar, the world of physical objects and living creatures.
> This is the realm accessible to us by sight and sound...
> But beneath these familiar phenomena lies another realm
> far more subtle and profound: a realm of consciousness,
> spirit [and] mind...We have bodies, but we also have, at the
> core of our being, in the depths of our minds, a center of
> transcendent awareness...[So] we are not only physical but
> also spiritual beings.[31]

Sages have called this "center of transcendent awareness" a variety of names, including *soul, spirit, the witness, inner luminosity, the Kingdom of God, Buddha nature,* and *the divine spark.* And they universally claim that it is related to and intimately connected with *the source* of all that is. In this way, we are each sacred.

OUR SENSE OF SPECIALNESS

These and other common attributes underlie our many differences and endow each of us with an inherent sense of *specialness*. As professor and writer Peter Vaill reminds us:

> The [individual], deeply aware of his or her own
> specialness, always confronts others who are deeply aware
> of their specialness…The specialness of myself right here,
> right now, is the sense that is most with each of us."[32]

From this sense of specialness arises our individual claim to person-hood: we realize at the most fundamental level that we are entitled to as much dignity, respect, and consideration as anyone else. Indeed, evolutionary psychologists claim that humans are acutely sensitive to being treated fairly or unfairly; that we are "hard-wired" for detecting injustice.

> The detection and punishment of injustice lie at the heart
> of human society. They are so important that people will
> actually harm their own short-term self interest to punish
> those they regard as behaving unfairly.[33]

One of life's central questions for us, then, is how to live and work together while reciprocally honoring one another's specialness. Sharif Abdullah, Director of the Commonway Institute, framed it this way:

> In a world of six billion humans and countless other beings,
> how can we create circumstances wherein each can flourish,
> without limiting the life expression of others? In short, how
> can we create a world that truly works for all?[34]

As a general guideline, the consensus wisdom across the centuries and cultures has been what we were taught as children—the *Golden Rule*. In the words of Jesus: "Do unto others as you would have them do unto you." This maxim is taught in one form or another in all of the world's major spiritual traditions, including Buddhism, Christianity, Confucianism, Hinduism, Islam, Judaism, and Taoism. As the United Nation's *Universal Declaration of Human Rights* states it: "All human beings are born free and equal in dignity and rights. They are endowed with reason and conscience and should act towards one another in a spirit of brotherhood."[35] People everywhere know that the *Golden Rule* and the *Declaration of Human Rights* ring true: we are each special, part of the human family, and mutually responsible for sustaining the network of care and responsibility that allows for a full and dignified human life. In the words of teacher and environmental activist Donella Meadows: "You are precious and special. So is everyone else, absolutely everyone. Act accordingly."[36]

WHAT DO PEOPLE WANT?

So what do people want out of life, anyway? It seems that regardless what part of the world we come from, we generally want the same thing—to be free of pain and fear, to be happy, to feel fulfilled, and to know at the deepest level that we have experienced "the rapture of being alive."[37]

Conventional consumer culture claims that happiness and fulfillment can be found primarily in the world of *things*, through money, power, sex, and fame. But while we certainly need material things in order to live comfortably and fully, having more of them does not necessarily bring more happiness and fulfillment. This fact has been demonstrated in the United States: while the average person's standard of living doubled between 1960 and 1990, the overall levels of happiness and life satisfaction did not increase "by one iota."[38] Philosopher and writer Eric Hoffer was evidently right: "We can never get enough of what we don't really need to be happy."[39] Apparently, we need a deeper understanding about ourselves and our drive toward happiness and fulfillment.

Psychologists and management theorists have created a variety of frameworks and lists that identify our common needs and wants, with the underlying premise being that we take action in the world in order to satisfy them. These needs and wants include items such as survival (including food, water, shelter, and health care), respect, a sense of belonging and affiliation, power, recognition, freedom, and fun.[40] And we strive for them at work and at home. While some theorists claim that satisfying these physical and psychological needs is the ultimate purpose of our lives, others have noted that they are actually means to achieving something else.

> I discovered that [people] usually began with wanting
> things from the outside, like protection, security, respect,

> love and approval from others, or success. Soon it became
> clear that if I kept asking, at some point (they) shifted from
> wanting something on the outside, to wanting a deep,
> inner, core feeling state. People described these states with
> many names, such as "oneness," "beingness," "a sense of
> peace," "OKness," and "love."[41]

These core states encompass ways of being that the Wisdom Traditions have long told us about: being fully present in the moment, rest-
ing in pure awareness; having an inner sense of peace and tranquility,
without worry, anxiety, or guilt; feeling unconditional love for self
and others that dissolves or transcends boundaries; having a sense of
being O.K. and intrinsically worthy, without the need to have or do
anything; feeling at one with all of existence, whole and complete.[42]
These states, which touch our deepest levels and yearnings, are universal human experiences and potentially available to each of us.
Indeed, the great mystics and seers claim that they are the manifested
essence of who or what we really are.

A World That Works for All

Ultimately, our human vocation is to evolve toward a wiser, more
liberated and luminous state of being. As we are able to do so, according to those who have gone before us, some wonderful things
happen. First, our hearts gradually open to a larger embrace of all
that is, and we come to increasingly care and be genuinely concerned
about the well being of others. Second, our worldview shifts, and we
come to see life less as a struggle and more as a dance. Moved by this
larger embrace and a sense of possibility in the dance, we increasingly strive to address the unfinished business of our society, doing
what we can to help the world work better for all. Thanks to this
dynamic, much of the wrong that people commonly do today will be
unthinkable tomorrow.

> The institution of slavery and segregation were maintained
> for hundreds of years, each generation being taught that
> these practices were normal. Similarly, we are currently
> engaged in behaviors that our grandchildren will consider

as barbaric as slavery: clearcutting forests, permitting virtually unregulated sales of cigarettes, tolerating hunger and homelessness, chemically manufacturing food, keeping people in economic slavery.[43]

Through enlightened living, people can create societies and workplaces that work for all. What are they like? According to Sharif Abdullah, they meet the following basic criteria.

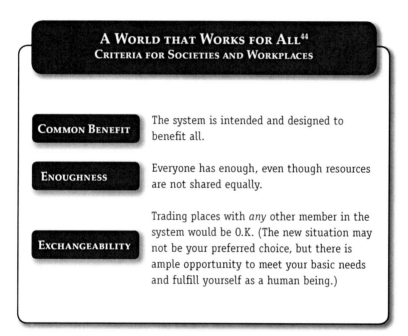

A WORLD THAT WORKS FOR ALL[44]
CRITERIA FOR SOCIETIES AND WORKPLACES

COMMON BENEFIT	The system is intended and designed to benefit all.
ENOUGHNESS	Everyone has enough, even though resources are not shared equally.
EXCHANGEABILITY	Trading places with *any* other member in the system would be O.K. (The new situation may not be your preferred choice, but there is ample opportunity to meet your basic needs and fulfill yourself as a human being.)

Work is about daily meaning
as well as daily bread…
for a sort of life rather than
a Monday-through-Friday sort of dying.

~ Studs Terkel

The consummation of work lies
not only in what we have done,
but who we have become
while accomplishing the task.

~ David Whyte

WORK

The dictionary defines work as "physical or mental effort exerted to do or make something...employment at a job...[or] making a living."[45] But work is more than that: it is also a vehicle for self-expression, growth, and fulfillment. Through work we can discover and live out who we really are and can be, both as individuals and as members of a community.[46]

OUR NOTIONS ABOUT WORK

In our society, people often consider work a necessary evil; they dislike working and do so only because they have to. Many people look forward to when they can stop working and retire. Even our language, which shapes our thoughts and actions, segregates work from a sense of enjoyment and play. Consider the following definitions [emphasis added].

> **play:** to amuse oneself, as by taking part in a
> game or sport; engage in recreation[47]

> **recreation:** refreshment in body or mind, *as after*
> *work,* by some form of play, amusement,
> or relaxation[48]

As humorist Mark Twain observed: "Work consists of whatever a body is obliged to do, and Play consists of whatever a body is not obliged to do."[49] Such attitudes have roots going back to the ancient belief that work is a necessary hardship, a mode of affliction that we must endure while here in this world.[50] Ancient myths expressed yearnings for a Golden Age, in which everything needed to support an effortless life would be readily available. The Greeks saw work as a curse, and the Hebrews considered it a punishment for sin, the result of being cast out of the Garden of Eden. According to early Christian doctrine, work, like disease and death, was the consequence of humankind's fall from grace. In order to serve as a punishment, it followed that work should be painful or unpleasant.

During the Industrial Age, the notion of work as a commodity was added to that of work as a hardship. People left their farms, craft shops, and families to go to work in factories. There the emphasis on mass production and efficiency resulted in jobs being reduced and divided into repetitive subtasks performed by individual, unskilled workers. "Work was separated out from all other aspects of life— home, family, pride of craftsmanship. Once isolated it became a pure commodity, purchased in blocks of time, one worker interchangeable for another."[51] This dehumanization of work was rationalized by the resulting material benefits, which were enormous. But these benefits were obtained at a high price: work became isolated from the rest of life, and the singular purpose of work became making a living. As a result, many of us now "work to eat, dreaming of escape, while real life happens on the weekend."[52]

A DIFFERENT VIEW OF WORK

Such notions about work are a menace to both ourselves and our society. There is, however, a significant body of wisdom that expands the meaning and purpose of work, thereby enriching our experience and our lives. For example:

- There can be no joy of life without joy of work.[53]

- The supreme accomplishment is to blur the line between work and play.[54]

- Work is just as important for personality, health, and growth as nutrients are for our bodies.[55]

- Work is an extension or reflection of your self.[56]

- There is a natural connection between a person's work life and all other aspects of life—we live only one life.[57]

- Work is inseparable from life, and only when we share with life the joy of creative work are we truly alive.[58]

- Work is meant to be the servant of humankind not the master.[59]

- Working is the natural response to being alive, our way of participating in the universe.[60]

- Work is love made visible.[61]

- Work is about creating, sustaining, and enlarging the possibilities of life.[62]

- Work is the use of consciousness to expand creation.[63]

- Work is our gift to the world.[64]

- Work will save the world…provided we know its real meaning and purpose.[65]

From these perspectives, work is about much more than just making a living. As one person said it: "I'm looking for something more than money out of work. I expect deep fulfillment and a little fun too." In the words of Claude Whitmyer, Director of graduate business programs at California Institute of Integral Studies:

> We long to do work that makes a difference and that contributes to our personal welfare, the welfare of those we love, and our community in general. We hunger for…work that satisfies our heart and still pays the bills.[66]

These yearnings relate to a sense of possibility that we each have about what it means to be alive and thriving as a human being. Thus, we can make a distinction between *a job* and *good work*—the former being something we do just to pay our bills, the latter being something that also provides a sense of purpose and engages our spirit.

THE PURPOSE OF WORK

With these perspectives in mind, we can identify several important purposes and functions of work.

Meet Our Basic Needs When we think of work we often think of "having a job." Interestingly, the word "job" originates from the Middle English *jobbe*, meaning "mouthful."[67] And so it is: through work we make a living; earning income to procure what we need for security, housing, food, clothing, education, and health care. Meeting these needs through work is a basic human right proclaimed for each of us under the United Nation's *Universal Declaration of Human Rights* as follows:

- the right to work, to free choice of employment, to favorable conditions of work, and to protection against unemployment

- the right to just and favorable remuneration, insuring for the individual and family an existence worthy of human dignity

- the right to a standard of living adequate for the health and well-being of the individual and the family[68]

Contribute to Society Through work we provide needed goods and services for one another. Being benefactors of the many advantages we enjoy in belonging to society, it is natural for us to want work that enables us to give back and to contribute to the welfare of others.

Promote Self-Expression Work and family are the two most significant social arenas where we express who we are and seek to achieve satisfaction and happiness.[69] And because most of our adult waking lives is spent at work, "the quality of our lives and the quality of our work-time are one and the same."[70] Work should, therefore, serve as an arena for us to "show up" in the world—expressing, sharing, and celebrating who we really are and want to be.

Support Our Development Learning and development are central to our process of becoming and to fulfilling ourselves as human beings. As the dominant activity of our adult waking lives, work needs to promote increasing levels of understanding, growth and development. In the process, we are not only creating better employees and citizens for today, we are also creating mentors and sages for tomorrow. This concept has long been espoused in the Wisdom Traditions, dating back over 2,000 years ago to Patanjali, the founder of yoga in ancient India. Summarizing this age-old principle, Edmond Szekely, philologist and co-founder of the International Biogenic Society, wrote:

> Work is the chief channel of expression for mind and soul...
> and therefore is not only the natural mode of individual
> and social development, but by far the best...The chief
> purpose of work is not to produce things, but to build the
> [person]. The chief purpose of work is not to make a living
> but to make a life—the greatest life for each individual.[71]

When work fulfills each of these purposes, it unleashes the power of the human spirit, encompassing the intangibles of meaning, commitment, and energy. Higher levels of creativity, quality, and productivity flow naturally as by-products of the experience. It follows that our work and workplaces be designed and managed accordingly—as vehicles and settings for meeting our basic material needs, contributing to a workable world, and promoting our self expression, enjoyment and growth. With this perspective in mind, the checklist on the following page can be used to evaluate the appropriateness of our workplace experience.

AN APPROPRIATE WORKPLACE EXPERIENCE
A CHECKLIST FOR INDIVIDUALS & ORGANIZATIONS

MEET BASIC NEEDS

People are meeting their basic needs for safety, security, and a material existence worthy of human dignity.

- ❑ **Wages.** People earn a "living wage," enabling them to procure decent housing in the local community, nutritious food, adequate clothing, transportation, education, and health care.

- ❑ **Safety.** People work in an environment that safeguards their health.

- ❑ **Trust.** People trust the leaders; they know that their well being is given appropriate weight and consideration in decision-making.

CONTRIBUTE TO SOCIETY

People are contributing to a meaningful and workable world by providing socially useful goods and services at reasonable cost.

- ❑ **Goods and Services.** The goods or services produced promote a workable and sustainable world.

PROMOTE ENJOYMENT, WELL-BEING & GROWTH

Jobs are designed for the wellness of the whole person, bringing together body, mind, and spirit.

- ❑ **Workplace Design.** The workplace is designed around human-scale mini-enterprises, or teams. There is variety in the work, the rules are flexible to accommodate individual needs, and people have as much autonomy as possible. Jobs incorporate authority, responsibility, wide scope, and multiple functions.

- ❑ **Communication.** People know what is going on in the organization, how their work contributes to the whole, and how they and the enterprise are doing.

- ❑ **Power and Influence.** People have power and influence. They participate in the management processes. This participation is voluntary and in accordance with the capacity of the individual.

- ❑ **Recognition and Rewards.** People are recognized for their contributions and equitably share in the material benefits of related gains.

- ❑ **Nature of the Experience.** Authenticity, self expression, acceptance, affiliation, power, freedom, and fun are all part of the experience.

- ❑ **Development Opportunities.** People have opportunities and support for both personal and professional growth. There are feedback systems, training programs, mentorships, and other mechanisms that support development.

Everybody can be great,
because everybody can serve.

~ Martin Luther King

Service is a way of
making deeper contact with
the interconnectedness of reality.

~ Arthur J. Deikman

SERVICE

M ost of us are employed in the service sector of the economy, so it is worth while investigating this aspect of work and work-places. *Service* is typically defined as "the act of helping someone or fixing something."

Service is not simply a New Age product and workplace phenomenon, but an activity and function that is woven throughout the fabric of human community. We support one another informally in countless ways—through "common courtesies, thoughtful gestures, [and] the simplest moments of human affirmation."[72] All of our major religions and schools of spiritual practice emphasize service. And no wonder: it is only through serving one another that we are able to meet our basic needs and fulfill ourselves as human beings.

SERVICE AS A SOCIAL EVENT

Providing a service is different from producing a commodity. For one thing, "a service cannot be centrally produced, inspected, stockpiled, or warehoused."[73]

> You can't put haircuts, or appendectomies, or flights to Cincinnati on a shelf and ring them up when a customer comes through the door. Neither can you offer sample sizes or 10-day free trials with a money-back guarantee.[74]

Service is created at the moment of delivery. And it cannot be recalled. It is a *social event*, usually involving some sort of human interaction between the giver and the recipient, or in workplace parlance, between the employee and the customer. Service, therefore, has two components: (1) performance of the task, and (2) the tone of the human interaction.[75] The perceived value of a service depends in part on the subjective nature of our experience in receiving it.

THE NORM OF MEDIOCRE SERVICE

Poor service is a common complaint in consumer-satisfaction surveys. But within the context of our culture, this should not be surprising. Consider the following:

Status In our society, as in all industrial cultures, high status is generally awarded to work that creates something that lasts, while low status is given to work that has to be done over and over again. Interestingly, this contemporary "hierarchy of work" contradicts the teachings of our major spiritual traditions. According to those teachings: "Doing work that has to be done over and over again helps us recognize the natural cycles of growth and decay, of birth and death, thereby remembering the dynamic order of the universe."[76] For this reason, the Wisdom Traditions placed great value on this kind of work.

Association In many people's minds, service is associated with being *servile*, defined as "abjectly submissive, slavish...relating to servitude or forced labor."[77] Service work, therefore, is often viewed as an undignified and unworthy occupation.

Values Our conventional culture emphasizes *materialism* and *accumulation*, while the essence of service is *sharing* and *giving away*. The Law of Scarcity, which dominates conventional culture and thinking, infers that "what we give away we lose."[79]

Rewards & Development While it seems commonsensical that the best services are provided by mature, satisfied people, service workers are usually the least trained and lowest paid employees. And to make matters worse, they are generally excluded from the management processes that affect and shape their workplace experience. However, as society and the organization treat the service staff, so, too, do they tend to treat the customers.[80]

These dynamics undermine the nature of the service experience for both customers and employees.

THE SERVICE MANAGEMENT TRIANGLE

Service management experts Karl Albrecht and Ron Zemke developed a three-fold approach and model for outstanding service—the

"Service Management Triangle."[81] This approach consists of an effective service strategy, user-friendly systems, and customer-friendly employees. The checklist below, based on their approach, can be used to evaluate the overall quality of services provided by an organization.

OUTSTANDING SERVICE[82]
A CHECKLIST FOR ORGANIZATIONS

EFFECTIVE SERVICE STRATEGY

❏ The enterprise provides a service that meets the needs of customers at a fair and reasonable price.

❏ The enterprise informs the customers about what to expect, and then meets or exceeds those expectations.

❏ The enterprise provides customers ample opportunities to provide input on what they need and to express how satisfied they are with the services provided, thereby enabling them to influence and shape outcomes.

ENGAGED STAFF

❏ Employees work with a consistently high level of concern for the needs of customers.

❏ Employees work in an efficient, effective, and timely manner.

❏ Employees are responsive, attentive, and genuinely willing to help the customers.

USER FRIENDLY SYSTEMS

❏ Forms, procedures and systems for both the customers and the employees are simple and kept to a minimum.

❏ As few employees as possible are involved in a transaction with a customer.

❏ Empoyees are empowered to override "the system" in unusual circumstances to meet the needs of the customer.

Formal leaders, including executives, managers, and supervisors, tend to think of service as something that occurs "out there," in the frontline arena. But they, too, are in service to others. As Albrecht and Zemke put it: "If you're not serving the customer, you'd better be serving someone who is."[83] In the best cases, leaders not only serve frontline employees, but they also serve the other stakeholders affected by the enterprise.

BEYOND HELPING AND FIXING

Serving is not always easy or natural for us, and there are often hidden motives involved when we *do* serve—a sense of obligation (helping because it is our job), a desire for personal gain (helping with thought of possible reward), or a need to "be good" (helping because of moral injunctions and programming we learned as children). When we serve from these places, conflicted feelings can arise that lead to disappointment, resistance, burnout, and resentment.[84] How, then, do we serve from a better place? Perhaps by remembering what author Hugh Prather wrote:

> I can be of no real help to another unless I see that the two
> of us are in this together, that all of our differences are
> superficial and meaningless, and that only the countless
> ways we are alike has any importance at all.[85]

From this perspective, serving is "a relationship among equals."[86] Rather than helping someone or fixing something, we are simply doing what is called for and needs to be done. Here, we share *all* of ourselves with another, and the roles of *giver* and *receiver* drop away.

What is ending is the idea that we are separate,
that one part of society can win at the expense of another,
that one nation has a right to war against another,
that one race has the right to dominate another,
that one sex has superiority over another,
that one species can dominate and destroy another species.

~ *Barbara Marx Hubbard*

ORGANIZATIONS

M ost of us work in organizations. But what are organizations? And what are their responsibilities, if any, to greater society? The dictionary defines *organizations* as "associations of people bound together into a body and sharing a common purpose."[87] They enable us to achieve something together that we would not be able to achieve individually. Organizations can be big or small, for-profit or non-profit, and they come in a variety of forms—companies, corporations, partnerships, associations, institutions, consortiums, networks, and government agencies.

A SOCIETY OF ORGANIZATIONS

Over the past century, responsibility for most social tasks has shifted from our families and local communities to organizations; where caring and exchange used to be done person-to-person by loved ones and neighbors, much of it is now done by and through organizations. "Every major social task, whether economic performance or health care, education or the protection of the environment, is today being entrusted to...organizations."[88] With transnational and multinational corporations, the reach of organizations stretches worldwide, affecting even indigenous peoples in the most remote parts of the world. This power now rivals that of many nations, with some corporations exercising "unparalleled control over global resources, labor pools, and markets."[89]

Management guru Peter Drucker noted that our organizations generally perform well, often achieving distinction in their focused areas of specialization. And he attributes that success to their narrow focus:

> All performing institutions of modern society are
> specialized. All of them are concerned only with their
> own task. The hospital exists to cure sick people. The fire
> department exists to prevent and extinguish fires. The
> business enterprise exists to satisfy economic wants...The
> strength of the modern pluralistic institution is that it is a
> single purpose institution.[90]

But organizations produce a wide range of outcomes—beneficial ones (e.g., needed goods and services, wages, and a living connection with others), as well as harmful ones (e.g., consumer junk, abandoned factories, and species extinction). The fact is, while organizations generally perform well *in their areas of specialization*, they tend to do so with remarkably little concern for the commons or the common good.

Much of the harm done by organizations goes unacknowledged because of their narrow focus and the lack of accountability to their various stakeholders. These *stakeholders*, or *constituents*, are all the people who either participate in, contribute to, or are affected by the enterprise and its actions. Organizations are not legally answerable to the vast majority of them; that is, there are no regulatory requirements to provide any sort of reckoning to them. This includes employees who dedicate their work lives to the enterprise, the local communities that provide needed infrastructure, and the future generations that are sharing their planet. The following, directed at corporations in particular but relevant to organizations in general, speaks to this issue.

> They are left largely unaccountable to the…constituents
> that contribute significantly to corporate [organizational]
> success or are affected by their actions—the stakeholders.
> As a consequence, employees, customers, suppliers,
> neighborhood communities, and greater society are too
> often sacrificed to the demands of the bottom line.[91]

Because each stakeholder has as much intrinsic value as another, the production of positive outcomes for some stakeholders with little regard for and at serious cost to other stakeholders is wrong. The fact is, organizations need to create and offer products and services in a manner that contributes toward a workable world, balancing the legitimate needs and rights of all those affected. James O'Toole, a leading expert on leadership and corporate ethics, has coined a term for this practice—*moral symmetry*.[92]

BUSINESS AND PROFIT

What does this mean for *business* organizations? After all, isn't the primary purpose of business to make a profit? While this is what

many owners and investors believe, there is a different way of thinking about business and profit. Consider the following:

- Profit is like oxygen—if you don't have enough you won't be
  around long, but if you think life is about breathing, you're
  missing something.[93]

- The fundamental goal of business is to improve the quality of
  life for all people.[94]

- *Narings liv* is the Swedish word for business. In English, *narings
  liv* literally means "nourishment for life."

- Business and company incorporation by charter were not
  invented, as we now assume, for individual self-interest and
  profit. They were invented for the common good. Financial
  profit was simply the incentive created so entrepreneurs would
  assume risk and take action that would lead them to act for the
  common good.[95]

- Free enterprise cannot be justified as being good for business. It
  can be justified only as being good for society.[96]

- Financial profit indicates precious little: simply that you have a
  product for which you have found a demand and that you can
  sell at a price in excess of your narrowly drawn fixed and
  variable costs. It says nothing about the nature of your product,
  and whether it serves or harms the wider community.[97]

According to these ways of thinking, the purpose of business is to
provide goods and services that promote the common good and do
not harm. Although profit may be an *end* for owners, it is the *means*
for society: in exchange for doing business in a way that contributes
to a workable world, owners are rewarded with profit. In other
words, being in business is a privilege not an entitlement, granted by
society and the community under the assumption that owners and
entrepreneurs will "obey the law, serve the common good, and cause
no harm."[98]

The one-dimensional focus on the "bottom line" that characterizes so many of our business organizations is based on the unchallenged tenet of maximizing returns to particular stakeholders, namely owners and shareholders. According to Marjorie Kelly, co-founder of *Business Ethics* magazine:

> This principle is reinforced by CEOs, *The Wall Street Journal*, business schools, and the courts. Indeed, maximizing returns to shareholders is almost universally accepted as a kind of divine, unchallengeable mandate.[99]

Kelly claims that this tenet is rooted in the aristocratic notion that "there are no limits to what the property-owning class might own or be entitled to."[100] While owners and shareholders certainly deserve fair returns on their investment, the *singular emphasis* on maximizing those returns often leads to actions that wrong other stakeholders— sending jobs to sweatshops overseas, demanding corporate welfare, refusing to give raises, using temporary workers to avoid paying benefits, wheedling tax breaks from government agencies, ignoring environmental safeguards, cutting down old-growth forests, destroying indigenous lands, et cetera.[101]

> Investors want increasing returns in the form of dividends and higher stock prices…Everything else, including the environment, employment, and quality of life is subordinated to this anonymous demand that is never satisfied.[102]

Conventional doctrine maintains that returns to most stakeholder groups are "losses" rather than "gains," "costs" rather than "benefits," "bad" rather than "good." But this is merely the parochial view of the dominant stakeholders—owners and shareholders. Other stakeholders would claim otherwise. For example, employees view rising wages as a gain; communities view taxes paid as a benefit; and future generations will likely view expenditures to safeguard the environment as a good. For a particular stakeholder group to view its own gains as benefits and *everything else* as losses, including benefits to other stakeholders, eventually undermines and destroys the commons within which the organization lives and prospers.

> [This] does not mean ignoring one's own interests or abandoning money and profit. It means taking the larger whole into consideration and not letting financial considerations assume an undue influence. The basis for [organizational] decision making becomes one's understanding that it is the whole, what we might call society and nature, that provides an enterprise's nourishment, health, and sustainability—not, as commonly believed, financial profit.[103]

THE PRACTICE OF MORAL SYMMETRY

Some organizations have reconsidered the one-dimensional focus on profit and embraced a more balanced framework known as the "triple bottom line."[104] This approach emphasizes not only *economic prosperity* for the enterprise, but also *social equity* and *environmental protection*—profits, people, and planet. It is an emerging paradigm for business and organizations in the 21st century, shifting our free enterprise system from *shareholder* capitalism to *stakeholder* capitalism—from a world that works for a few to a world that works for all.

> For organizations to prosper over the long term, they must contribute something. And the more they can contribute on multiple dimensions, they more they're likely to prosper. Those multiple dimensions include communities, customers, and employees.[105]

What do the triple bottom line and moral symmetry look like in practice? Well, it is different from the typical approach of maximizing returns for a few privileged constituents. The table on the next page provides a basic checklist of legitimate needs and rights for the various stakeholders. As it indicates, even "win/win" approaches are not enough. What we really need are "wins" for each stakeholder group; that is, "win/win/win/win/win/win" approaches.

STAKEHOLDER NEEDS & RIGHTS
A CHECKLIST OF LEGITIMATE CLAIMS ON THE ORGANIZATION

OWNERS & SHAREHOLDERS

- ❏ Reasonable profit (for-profit) or net operating surplus (non-profit)
- ❏ Continuity in organizational capacity to provide goods and services, including the ability to change and adapt
- ❏ Adherence by employees to policies and procedures necessary for safeguarding the investment and sustaining the enterprise

CUSTOMERS

- ❏ Quality goods and services at reasonable prices
- ❏ Goods and services that do not harm

EMPLOYEES

- ❏ A living wage, adequate for purchasing food, clothing, housing, health care, and education
- ❏ A safe and healthy working environment
- ❏ Basic human rights, including respect, freedom for self-expression, and non-discriminatory workplace practices
- ❏ Meaningful work contributing to a workable world
- ❏ Gainsharing, resulting from and proportional to contributions
- ❏ Opportunities for both personal and professional growth

SUPPLIERS

- ❏ Information that enhances or threatens continuity as a provider
- ❏ Fair remuneration to meet legitimate claims of its own stakeholders

COMMUNITY & SOCIETY

- ❏ Goods and services that meet legitimate human needs, promote the common good, and do not harm
- ❏ Efficient (doing the most with the least) and effective (doing the right things) use of resources
- ❏ Good citizenship, including respect for local culture

FUTURE GENERATIONS

- ❏ Sustainable use of resources, including preservation of the scope and diversity of living systems and their capacity for self-renewal
- ❏ Preservation of options for meeting future needs

Ethicist John Rawls developed a simple approach for practicing moral symmetry. It employs what he calls, "a veil of ignorance" for making decisions in a manner that we could live with, regardless of which stakeholder we are.[106] The following table outlines this approach and process.

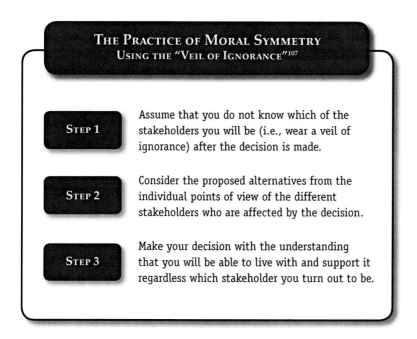

THE PRACTICE OF MORAL SYMMETRY
USING THE "VEIL OF IGNORANCE"[107]

STEP 1
Assume that you do not know which of the stakeholders you will be (i.e., wear a veil of ignorance) after the decision is made.

STEP 2
Consider the proposed alternatives from the individual points of view of the different stakeholders who are affected by the decision.

STEP 3
Make your decision with the understanding that you will be able to live with and support it regardless which stakeholder you turn out to be.

Lastly, Ken Blanchard and Norman Vincent Peale offer a practical check for ethical decision making. Their approach is to simply ask: "How will this decision and action make me feel if *all of the specifics* were made public in the local newspaper?"[108]

STAKEHOLDER PARTICIPATION

But how do we know what the various stakeholders want or need in a particular situation? Simple. We ask them. Although they rarely do so, organizations can directly involve their stakeholders in deliberations, decision-making, and implementation. Several proven social technologies are available that can be used, including *dialogue, future-search conferences,* and *open-space gatherings*. These approaches use individual views as powerful resources for discovering more compelling and inclusive alternatives.

Dialogue

Dialogue is a "conversation with a center but no sides," involving from a few to 40 or 50 people.[109] Used by indigenous people, the early Greeks, and others, it is a form of collective inquiry into the assumptions and thinking that underlie our individual opinions and positions. Through a process of mutual discovery over two hours or two days, new insights and shared wisdom emerge that affect behavior and illuminate new possibilities for joint action and support.[110]

> In dialogue, individuals gain insights that simply could not be achieved individually…[The] group explores complex difficult issues from many points of view…The result is a free exploration that brings to the surface the full depth of people's experience and thought, and yet can move beyond their individual views.[111]

Future Search Conferences

Future Search is a planning process involving up to 60 or 70 people, comprising representatives from each of the organization's stakeholder groups. Participants work together in a two or three-day structured format to review the past, explore the present, envision desired outcomes, identify common ground, and develop action plans. The process can be used to address a specific issue or develop and work toward a desired future.[112]

Open-Space Gatherings

Open Space is a group-planning process involving from a few to upwards of 1,000 participants. It is "particularly powerful when nobody knows the answers and the ongoing participation of a number of people is required to deal with the questions."[113] The process is designed to address specific issues through a self-organizing approach based on personal responsibility and choice.

World Café Process

Incorporating elements from the preceding venues, the World

Café format enables large numbers of people to connect and process particular issues. Options include the use of several gatherings over different times.[114]

Although conventional thinking holds that it is impractical or impossible to work through challenging issues with large groups of people having different perspectives, experience using the above methods has demonstrated otherwise. Indeed, the most satisfying and effective outcomes are usually achievable only through such venues.

Each of us affected by a decision has a moral claim on the decision maker: as stakeholders we each deserve nothing less than serious consideration when being affected by an organization. This includes owners and shareholders affected by threats to their investment, customers affected by harmful products, employees affected by mergers and downsizing, suppliers affected by competitiuon and discontinued product lines, local communities affected by plant relocation and closings, indigenous people affected by exploitation and extraction of natural resources, and future generations affected by non-sustainable environmental practices and the degradation of living systems. Organizations—both for-profits and non-profits—are deserving of our commitment and support to the extent that they extend and balance such care and consideration to each of their stakeholders.

The aim of life can only be
to increase the sum of freedom
and responsibility to be found in
every person and in the world.

~ Albert Camus

Freedom is participation in power.
~ Cicero

GOVERNANCE & MANAGEMENT

G overnance is about having and exercising authority over an enterprise, institution, or organization. It is the *meta*system which controls and mediates all the other systems. Standard texts and dictionaries inform us that *governing* encompasses the power to establish strategic direction, make policy, administer affairs, command others, and exact obedience.[115] But this conventional framing speaks little to the other possibilities that lie hidden within this all-important function. Consider the following definition by Patricia McLagan and Christo Nel, co-founders of the Democracy and Work Institute:

> Governance...refers to the way in which the stakeholders of an institution [government, community, business or family] live out their power, rights, and responsibilities.[116]

Thus, we are reminded that governance is ultimately about the way we choose to live together. In terms of those choices, governance may be either *authoritarian* or *participatory*, and for some time now society has been undergoing a shift from the former to the latter.

FROM DOMINATION TO PARTNERSHIP

For over three thousand years, the prevailing form of governance in our economic, political, and social institutions has been authoritarian. McLagan and Nel describe this type of governance as follows:

> In authoritarian systems, power and rights are concentrated in a small group whose members exercise power over others...[This] elite group rules, thinks, and determines goals and resource use...The majority of the population follows orders and implements policies...Coercion, power over others, threats and fears of loss of position or access, and financial carrots and sticks keep people in line and ensure that they implement the leader's vision of the institution's purpose and goals.[117]

Although authoritarian leaders do not like to talk about it, most of us are acutely aware that authoritarian systems are relatively ineffective and morally inferior.

> In authoritarian systems, citizens, employees, and even customers are essentially subservient or—worse— disenfranchised and disempowered. The relationships between authoritarian leaders and their constituencies can be either dependent or hostile. In the more benign forms of autocracy, managers are institutional parents, while employees are loyal organizational children.[118]

Over the past few centuries, people and societies have been moving away from authoritarian systems. This trend has resulted in our democratic government, the prohibition of slavery, and progress toward the emancipation of women. It has also been evident in a variety of workplace innovations over the last several decades—the Scanlon Plan, quality of work life initiatives (QWL), employee involvement (EI), quality circles, employee stock-ownership programs (ESOPs), total quality management (TQM), self-directed teams (SDTs), and Lean Manufacturing. Although we often experience these innovations within a "flavor-of-the-month" context, they are nothing less than part of a long-term evolution and fundamental shift in society's approach to institutional governance—from authoritarian to participatory—from domination to partnership. As McLagan and Nel claim: "Participation is the great governance trend...[and] this is crossover time from one form of governance to another."[119]

POWER

At the heart of governance and human relationship lies *power*, which is the measure or amount of social control or influence that a person or group has. As philosopher Bertrand Russell noted: "The fundamental concept in social science is power. In the same sense in which energy is the fundamental concept in physics."[120] So, just as we need to understand and work with *energy* in physics, so too do we need to understand and work with *power* in our social systems and society.

Authoritarian systems are built on the power of *coercion*, which is exclusive: one person or group has the ability to force other people to do things they may or may not want to do. The central issue in authoritarian systems is how formal leaders can hold and exercise power over others without ultimately sharing it. Thus, behind the rational and sincere appearance of most bosses lies intimidation and threats of punishment. Because coercion denies that which is most human in us—our free will and the ability to choose—we recoil from and rebel against it, no matter where we find it. This issue is generally not discussable and manipulation is, therefore, endemic. As the writer and psychiatrist R. D. Laing put it:

> They are playing a game. They are playing at not playing a
> game. If I show them I see they are, I shall break the rules
> and they will punish me. I must play their game, of not
> seeing I see the game.[121]

Participatory systems, on the other hand, are based on the power of *mutual influence,* which is reciprocal: "If I want to influence you, I must be willing to let you influence me."[122] Each person is able to influence and be influenced by others in choosing what they want to do or support. Through this exercise of free will and choice, we are able to be authentic and fully human, creating both ourselves and our world. The primary issue in participatory systems is how we can make ourselves vulnerable to being influenced by others while meeting our own basic needs and preserving our sense of self-identity.

Experience with participatory systems dispels a common misconception we tend to have about power—that it is material and finite, a "zero-sum" resource that must be taken from one person in order to give to another. "Bosses worry that if they give power to the workers, they, themselves, will lose power. [But] the exact opposite is true."[123]

> Enlightened leaders consider power to be infinite, and
> valuable only insofar as it is given away…In this view,
> power can be likened to a candle. If my candle is lit, and I
> share the flame with those around me, I have lost nothing;
> indeed, I have *gained* because of the increased light and
> warmth generated by multiple candles.[124]

THE BOSS SYSTEM

Although society has been moving toward participatory systems, authoritarian governance remains predominant in our organizations and workplaces. Related artifacts include executive privileges and shameful compensation packages. The average big-company CEO, for example, now makes more than three hundred times what the average worker makes.[125] But the most pervasive and problematic artifact is the boss structure and reporting relationship. This frame-work—in which one person, the *boss*, holds unilateral power and authority over others, the *subordinates*—remains entrenched throughout our workplaces.

> No management system is more firmly fixed…than that
> of the boss. Bosses are in charge of workers; they tell them
> what, when, and how to do their job. They have the power
> to reward them for doing a good job and to punish them for
> not doing what they are told to do.[126]

The *boss system* permeates our enterprises from the frontline to the boardroom in both for-profit and non-profit organizations. And it has been this way for so long that people rarely question it. Its roots can be traced at least as far back as the Abrahamic religious traditions (i.e., Judaism, Christianity and Islam) in which the universe and humankind were made by "God the Father." This God was the ultimate boss, endowed with infinite wisdom and the love, but tempered with judgment and the threat of punishment for those who disobeyed. Feudal lords and monarchs later cast themselves in similar roles with their serfs and subjects. Just prior to the Industrial Revolution, the boss was usually the father in either farming or a cottage trade. Concerned about both the people involved and the task at hand, this *father boss* managed with both the love of a parent and the authority to discipline.[127] With industrialization, people left their family-based enterprises to go to work for owners in the factories. There, the managerial role evolved from the father-boss concept into paternalism, and then later to the *professional boss*—a bureaucratic one—rational and fair but relatively uncaring about subordinates.[128] Indeed, caring came to be considered a dangerous contaminant to the managerial decision-making process, which was supposed to be aligned primarily with the material interests of the owners.

The prevailing boss structure works to the disadvantage of just about everyone—subordinates, the organization, and, surprisingly, even bosses themselves. The one-sided vulnerability of subordinates results in a preoccupation with safety, security, and other self-interests. Their personal experience makes it quite clear that being safe or getting ahead is dependent on obeying the boss—performance assessments and job references being cases in point. While subordinates want to make meaningful contributions to the enterprise, they also want to make their mortgage payments. Since they are at the mercy of their boss and ultimately stand alone in the system, the practical wisdom is for them to avoid personal responsibility (in case anything goes wrong), restrain self-expression, and maintain an appearance of loyalty to their boss. "We do whatever it takes to stay on the good side of whoever controls our livelihood."[129] Authenticity and truth-telling are sacrificed for safety and security; petty striving for personal gain is sanctioned over service to others; our sense of adventure and risk-taking are traded for politics and bureaucracy.

Because bosses have bosses and are subordinates too, they "behave upwards" in the same manner. But they are affected by the system in other ways as well. As the grandfather of the empowerment movement, Robert K. Greenleaf, insightfully wrote:

> To be a lone chief atop a pyramid is abnormal and corrupting. None of us is perfect by himself [or herself] and all of us need the help and correcting influence of close colleagues. When a person is moved atop a pyramid he or she no longer has colleagues, only subordinates…Normal communication patterns become warped…The pyramidal structure weakens informal links, dries up channels of honest reaction and feedback, and creates limiting chief-subordinate relationships…The man or woman at the top often suffers from a very real loneliness.[130]

The term "lone chief atop a pyramid" can apply to *any* leader, manager, or supervisor holding unilateral authority over subordinates. By holding such power, an individual becomes isolated from the correcting influence of the surrounding community.

> The policy that the boss always has his door open sounds fine, but unless a subordinate is about to resign, he is not likely to go through that open door to suggest that his superior is handling the work in ways that are inefficient, is creating unnecessary difficulties for his subordinates, or is unfair or unreasonable. Moreover, the worse the situation, the more difficult it is for a subordinate to communicate these facts to his chief.[131]

Most of us are all too familiar with how the boss system handicaps and penalizes an enterprise. Because of the differences in position power and vulnerability, the organization is typically stratified into *Tops, Middles,* and *Bottoms*.[132] Bottoms avoid responsibility, withold information, and herd together for self-protection. They view bosses as "one of them," rather than "one of us." Meanwhile, the Middles are torn to align themselves with either the Bottoms below (their subordinates) or the Tops above (their bosses). And the Tops, isolated from those below, compete with one another to protect or promote their assigned "organizational chimney." In the words of psychiatrist and author William Glasser: "The worst feature of boss-management is that it always results in [people] becoming adversaries...It occurs at every level."[133]

Do bosses consciously conspire to create such outcomes? Of course not. Rather, the nature of the system simply makes it difficult for the human spirit to manifest and, in the end, everyone loses. In the words of social commentator Sam Keen: "I know of no more radical critique of economic life than the observation that nowhere in the vast literature of management is there a single chapter on friendship."[134] But it is rare to find a boss who fully comprehends the limitations of the prevailing authoritarian model, and even rarer to find one who is willing to consider giving up this approach. Even though most bosses resent having to practice the time-consuming and energy-draining "arts" of politics and bureaucracy, they see no workable or realistic alternatives. Nevertheless, such alternatives—participatory ones—do exist.

THE FUNCTIONS OF MANAGEMENT

Before outlining what participatory governance looks like in the workplace, it is helpful to review what the boss does in the traditional system. This work of the boss is generally referred to as *management*, which is defined as "a process by which a cooperative group directs their actions toward common goals."[135] The primary purpose of management, then, is to combine and connect the various actions and efforts into an integrated whole that effectively accomplishes the goals of the enterprise. The management functions are fundamental to all types of cooperative endeavors, and they are found at all organizational levels. Experts generally agree that they include the following:

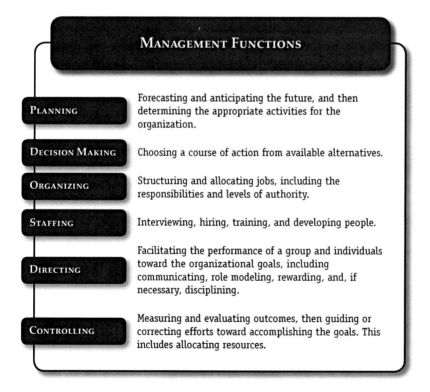

MANAGEMENT FUNCTIONS

PLANNING — Forecasting and anticipating the future, and then determining the appropriate activities for the organization.

DECISION MAKING — Choosing a course of action from available alternatives.

ORGANIZING — Structuring and allocating jobs, including the responsibilities and levels of authority.

STAFFING — Interviewing, hiring, training, and developing people.

DIRECTING — Facilitating the performance of a group and individuals toward the organizational goals, including communicating, role modeling, rewarding, and, if necessary, disciplining.

CONTROLLING — Measuring and evaluating outcomes, then guiding or correcting efforts toward accomplishing the goals. This includes allocating resources.

The performance of these functions aims at integrating and sustaining the organizational enterprise as a whole. While authoritarian systems reserve the management functions for a relatively few people at the top of organizations or units, an impartial review suggests that most people in an organization can be so engaged.

> People who act as adults in everyday life—who manage families, serve as PTA presidents, run Little Leagues, and accomplisha wider range of other adult tasks—surely deserve a chanceand encouragement to assume similar responsibility in their workplaces.[136]

Participatory Governance

To effectively govern and manage an enterprise, people need information, knowledge, power, and rewards. Participatory systems, therefore, move these resources and capacities further "down" in organizations, enabling people to collaborate in doing what the boss used to do.[137] What does a participatory governance system look like? According to research on highly effective organizations, "the [enterprise] consists most basically of a structure of groups, linked together by overlapping memberships into a pyramid through which the work flows."[138] While effective participatory systems can vary considerably, they typically include a mix of the following elements.

Teams & Work Groups The basic organizational unit, whether at the frontline or in the boardroom, is the team or work group. The members have a mix of complementary capacities needed to do the work of the team, which fall into three categories:

(1) technical and functional expertise;
(2) problem-solving and decision-making skills; and,
(3) interpersonal skills related to group process.[139]

The team operating dynamic is an open forum in which each member freely participates as they choose. People report to their team as a whole rather than to a single boss, unless they prefer otherwise. The performance of any individual on the team thereby becomes the business of the entire team. Importantly, teams are linked organizationally to other teams both horizontally and vertically by overlapping representation and other means. This "linkage" entails a continuous process of monitoring and assuring a mutual good fit and synergy of the efforts of the teams and their subunits.[140] Other mechanisms for linkage includes team subgroups, task forces, ad hoc and informal discussions and dialogues, friendships, mentorships, workshops, and retreats.

Partnership & Influence People are partners and collaborators in the enterprise. This partnership means that "Whatever we're in, we both created…[and] we're both responsible for creating tomorrow."[141] Individuals have meaningful influence on their teams, and teams have meaningful influence on the system—upwardly, laterally, and downwardly.[142]

Clear Boundaries The governing ideas of the enterprise are clearly stated, including the mission, values, and goals. Everyone knows what is expected of them, thereby fostering a sense of "responsible autonomy" in which both individuals and teams decide for themselves what to do but are held accountable for the outcomes.[143] The rights and responsibilities of each member are clearly delineated, as well as how rules are made and enforced. Items addressed include:

> [T]he broad parameters of one's role, rights, and obligations
> of community participation, structures for decision-making
> and distribution of power and economic rewards, processes
> for individual and group evaluation, means of dispute
> resolution, and guidelines for selecting and dismissing
> leaders and members.[144]

Both individuals and teams are formally chartered and committed to sharing power and authority in good faith. This *good faith* has to do with both intentions and behavior, and can be defined as: "demonstrating a sincere commitment to the well-being of the enterprise."[145]

Volition & Choice As much as possible, organizational systems and processes are based on free will and choice—no one is coerced into doing something. Decision-making is done by *consensus,* which is defined as "every member being willing to accept and support the decision as a good one for the group and enterprise, even if it doesn't represent their personal first choice."[146] Voting is discouraged for important reasons. First, it is a form of coercion in which the majority forces the minority to do or support something they do not want. Second, voting typically leads to factions in the group and "horse trading" across issues. Lastly, in the words of oral historian Paula Underwood, "In the wisdom of the majority, the wisdom of the minority is lost."[147]

Countervailing Power With consensus decision-making and open access to decision-making bodies, every person in the system has influence and power. No one person has unilateral power over another, and there is protection against the arbitrary use of power. Individuals and teams are able to pursue issues and appeal decisions through higher organizational levels openly and without fear of retribution.

Alignment of Systems Organizational structures and systems are aligned with participatory governance.[148] Leadership and governance processes are, therefore, accomplished through pluralistic, egalitarian, open-ended exchanges.[149] Employees, are at the center of organizational decision making.[150] Management processes related to strategies, plans, initiatives, budgets, goals, feedback, staffing, and rewards are all determined and accomplished in participatory ways. As much as possible, decisions are made by those most affected and closest to the scene of the action.[151]

Servant Leadership The formal leaders are "firsts among equals" rather than bosses.[152] As such, they have accountability without unilateral control or compliance.[153] Although they are expected to provide a reckoning on outcomes and are therefore at risk, they cannot coerce others to do things they do not want to do. In decision-making, the formal leaders are simply "other voices at the table." They serve the enterprise as coaches, facilitators, role models ("walking the talk"), mentors, experts, and partners, thereby creating capacity in people and the system. As a group, they form a *leadership alliance* that involves as many people as possible in the work that has traditionally been done by authoritarian managers.[154] They also hold the enterprise and system in trust as an act of stewardship and service, representing the legitimate interests of all the stakeholders.

Acceptance & Support Everyone matters: the organization honors and actively supports the dignity, rights, and responsibilities of each member. And each person is accepted and valued for who he or she is. Individuals are thereby supported in being *authentic*, bringing all of who they are into the workplace. This makes true or deep relationship possible.[155] It is also recognized that both individuals and teams need self-understanding and a wide range of social and technical skills to manage and govern the enterprise effectively. There is, therefore, *considerable* support for both personal and professional development.

Openness & Transparency The system is an "open book": there are no secrets. Information about revenue, income, expenses, individual performance, team performance, salaries, merit pay, and other business metrics is readily available. Processes and decisions are handled above-board and involve those affected as well as those who will have to make things work. Agendas and meeting minutes are freely shared. Regardless of the organizational level, team meetings are open to the organizational community for access and observation by others.

Participatory governance is based on mutual caring and support rather than fear and politics, making it safe for people to be authentic, assume responsibility, and grow. As a system matures, the levels of fairness, social justice, community, and sense of well being all increase. People become partners in co-creating the enterprise and come to value and appreciate both the opportunity and the experience. The focus is on contribution and service rather than on security and accumulation.

With participation, people come to realize and believe that what they do *does* make a difference—that they *do* matter, and that they *can* change their part of the world.[156] Resulting increases in both productivity and quality are well documented: studies have concluded that meaningful participation has a significant, positive effect on productivity, almost never being negative or neutral.[157] What do we mean by *meaningful* here? We mean "the power to affect the life of the community," where the privilege of participation results in personal roles and actions that can have consequences for the organization as a whole.[158]

> The move toward participation as the prevailing form of
> governance in the workplace and the world continues...
> Its moral superiority and its capacity to outperform
> authoritarian systems guarantee its advance.[159]

So what does participation look like in practice? And how does one go about living it out? The text box and statement on the facing page, crafted almost three decades ago by research scientist David G. Bowers, is a down-to-earth, operational description for the practice of workplace participation.

THE WORKPLACE AS COMMUNITY

Participatory systems result in workplaces that are radically different from authoritarian ones. Instead of a stratified society of Tops, Middles, and Bottoms, something else is evoked—something called "community." *Community* is defined as "life in association with others,"[161] The word is derived from the Latin *com munere*, which means "to give among each other."[162] In our culture, community is often framed as a trade-off with *individuality* in a zero-sum equation—the more community the less individuality, and vice versa. But speaking from the Native American Wisdom Traditions, Paula Underwood claims otherwise:

> The Community is the seedbed of Individuality...In my
> tradition, that Community is considered wise which allows
> maximum possible learning, growth, and development to

How Participation Works[160]

The elements of participation…consist of (*a*) group, rather than [person-to-person], methods of supervision, (*b*) the open flow of information in all directions (with immunity from ridicule or vindictiveness), and (*c*) the ability of all parties to exercise a measure of influence over outcomes.

A [leader] attempting to follow a participative pattern typically presents to his group in a regular staff meeting a problem which faces them collectively, and before any decision has been made about it, encourages all views, makes his own available without presenting it in such a way as to override others, and develops those processes which result in the pooling of all relevant information. From this he helps the group to develop an integrative solution to the problem at hand, one to which they are all, including himself, willing to commit themselves.

In making decisions in this participative group fashion, there are facts, such as deadlines, minimum financial conditions as to earnings or reserves, or the like, which cannot be ignored if the organization is to achieve its objectives. It is the task of the [leader] to be fully aware of these *situational requirements*, and to make his subordinate group aware of them as well. In making decisions, he and his group should never lose sight of them.

[The leader's] responsibility is not to make the best decisions, but to so structure and guide events that *the best possible decisions are made*…Acquiring the knack of doing [this] is, first and foremost a task of simply *doing* it, and learning by the doing.

each and every one of its Individual members…[And] that
Individual is wise who gives to his, to her, Community.
However big and strong you may be, sooner or later you
will need help from your Community. If you haven't
nurtured your Community in some adequately relevant
way as you've gone along, it may not be there when you
need it. So you see how it is…If you neglect the Individuals,
it will cost you as a Community. If you neglect the
Community, it will cost you as Individuals.[163]

From this perspective, community is first and foremost about personal growth and development. In the words of consultant and
author Juanita Brown: "Community is the soil from which things
grow."[164] As community members, therefore, we are called upon to:
(1) understand what we need from the community, (2) accept or take
what is freely given, and (3) contribute what we can in return. By
doing so, we create a common gift and quality of life for one another—
the opportunity to discover and live out who we are and who we can
be as individuals and human beings. This is our shared birthright
and our common destiny in community.

Conventional doctrine holds that the purpose of workplaces is different from that of communities—the former being to complete tasks for
the production and exchange of goods and services; the latter being
to create a satisfying and meaningful life experience. With participatory governance, however, these realms are merged; goods and
services are produced through a mutually satisfying and meaningful
life experience.

The way work gets done (including sociability, learning,
participation, responsibility, and fairness) is as important
as the final results…In the end, what participants treasure
is not simply the enterprise's success but also the personal
growth, development, satisfaction, and fulfillment they
receive from being part of the process.[165]

The workplace-as-community approach represents a change in
worldview from organization as "lean machine" to organization as

"vital organism."[166] And when it manifests, both the human spirit and organizational performance soar; workplace communities are successful enterprises of mutual endeavor:

> The distinguishing feature of many of these organizations is that all employees are participants in the re-creation of their organizations into entities that serve all members... Teamwork, learning, flexibility, caring, a sense of belonging, and gainsharing, for example, are qualities to be found in community...When community is built, bureaucracy is replaced. Power shifts to negotiated relationships and to teams and networks. Communications are open and authentic. Feedback is continual, occurring during the normal course of doing one's work...The operative environment that is established is inclusive and responsive...The community model is a dynamic system of people at work. [167]

The table on the following page—*The Spectrum of Governance*—provides an overview of how authoritarian workplaces differ from participatory ones. Assuming a world of polar opposites, where would you rather work—in a *conventional organization* or in a *workplace community*?...Where would you want your loved ones to work?... Why?...Which system would you trust more?...In which system would you contribute most to the enterprise?...Where would you judge *your* workplace to be on a continuum ranging from conventional organization to workplace community?

THE SPECTRUM OF GOVERNANCE

FROM AUTHORITARIAN...............TO PARTICIPATORY

POWER	
• Control is concentrated in a small group of people or individuals who hold unilateral power over others.	• Power is shared.
• Decisions are made and orders are issued downward.	• Decisions are made on a consensus basis.

SOCIAL SYSTEM & PROCESSES	
• People are divided into Tops, Middles, and Bottoms. Negative politics are common.	• There is a sense of belonging and caring.
• Participation in management processes is restricted to Tops and some Middles.	• There are opportunities for everyone to participate in ways that potentially have consequences for all.

MEMBERSHIP	
• Membership is based primarily on performance.	• Membership is based primarily on intentions and good faith effort.

REWARDS & RISKS	
• Risks, sacrifices, and gains are not equitably shared. Tops receive greater rewards.	• Risks, sacrifices, and gains are equitably shared.

CLIMATE & CULTURE	
• Motivational forces are based on fear and self-protection.	• Motivational forces are based on love and mutual respect.
• There is little to no trust. Hostility and dissatisfaction are common.	• People trust one another and the system. Attitudes are favorable.

COMMUNICATION & INFORMATION	
• Self expression is restrained. Many things are not discussable.	• People are authentic. Everything is discussable.
• Information is available on a "need to know" basis only. And the formal leaders determine who needs to know.	• The information system is an "open book." All information is available as requested to members, and stakeholders.
• Information is distorted and filtered.	• Communication flows freely upward, downward, and laterally.

OUTCOMES	
• High costs and low productivity	• Low costs and high productivity
• Mediocre living	• Ecstatic living

*The obligation of accepting a position of power
is to be, above all else, a good human being.*

~ Peter Block

*Leadership is an act of giving.
Giving what?
Just giving.
Giving as a way of life.
Giving whatever the situation needs.
Giving yourself.
Giving comes naturally when you care deeply.
It's another face of love.*

~ Jack Hawley

LEADERS &
LEADERSHIP

The term *leader* conjures up a remarkable range of images and possibilities. Consider the following, for example: Alexander the Great, Eleanor Roosevelt, Hitler, Jesus, Joan of Arc, Genghis Khan, Martin Luther King, Rosa Parks, Stalin, and Susan B. Anthony. All were great leaders in an historical sense, but they left astoundingly different legacies—ranging from the inspirational to the horrifying.

WHAT IS A LEADER?

The standard dictionary defines *leader* as "one who is in charge or in command of others."[168] Selected individuals are invested by the system with this *authority*, the right to give orders and the power to exact obedience. These *formal leaders* are officially designated to be in charge of our institutions and organizations, and are supposedly held accountable for performance and outcomes. Thus, formal leadership is not so much about rank, privilege, and rewards, as it is about *responsibility*.[169] Peter Drucker, the father of modern management theory, claimed that being a formal leader is what has traditionally been meant by the term *professional*.[170] And the first responsibility of a professional was spelled out 2,500 years ago in the Hippocratic oath of the Greek physicians—"Above all, not knowingly do harm."

In the workplace, formal leaders have job titles such as CEO, director, executive officer, foreman, manager, owner, president, vice-president, superintendent, and supervisor. As subordinates, we commonly refer to them as "the boss" and people assume such individuals are leaders. But does having the power of command really make them leaders? Probably no more so than having a hammer makes someone a carpenter.

At the most basic level, a leader is "someone who has followers."[171] Since the term *followers* implies an act of free will and choice, a leader can also be defined as "a person that other people follow not by force but voluntarily."[172] Thus, a leader is different from a *ruler* or a *tyrant*. So there is something more to leadership than just being in charge or having command. In pondering what that "something" might be, consider the following:

- We lead by being human.[173]

- To become a leader one must first become a human being.[174]

- Enlightened leadership is about service, not selfishness.[175]

- The basic task of leadership is to increase the standard of living and the quality of life for all stakeholders.[176]

- Leadership: (Gaelic origin) quest, or journey.

- To lead, one must follow.[177]

- The art of leadership: liberating people to do what is required of them.[178]

- The task of leadership is to help the followers go where they want to go.[179]

- Leadership is not so much the exercise of power itself as the empowerment of others.[180]

- The great leader is seen as servant first.[181]

- Leadership is a…condition of the heart.[182]

Consistent with these perspectives, we come to our last and probably most helpful definition:

> Leadership is about creating, day by day, a domain in which we and those around us continually deepen our understanding of reality and are able to participate in shaping our future.[183]

While most definitions focus on the *what* of being a leader, there is also a *why* and a *how* of being a leader. Although often ignored, these are as important as the what. And the last definition touches upon that. As the Chinese philosopher Lao Tsu noted over two thousand years ago, principle and process are inseparable: "What happens arises out of how it happens."[184] More recently, playwright and Czechoslovakian President Vaclev Havel stated it this way: "There is only one way to strive for decency, reason, responsibility, sincerity, civility, and tolerance, and that is decently, reasonably, responsibly, sincerely, civilly, and tolerantly."[185]

THE LEGITIMACY OF LEADERSHIP

Leaders hold and exercise extraordinary power. They are thereby uniquely positioned to positively or negatively shape the nature of our workplaces, organizations, and world. In the words of teacher and activist Parker Palmer:

> [A] leader is a person who has an unusual degree of power to project on to other people his or her shadow, or his or her light...to create the conditions under which other people must live and have their being—conditions that can be as illuminating as heaven or as shadowy as hell.[186]

This raises questions about the nature of *legitimate* leadership, which has to do with intentions, means, and ends. *Intentions* relate to the "why" (the reason and meaning for doing something), *means* relate to the "how" (methods used to get things done), and *ends* relate to the "what" (desired goals and outcomes). Each of these need to be sanctioned as "appropriate and right" for a leader or leadership group to be legitimate. But sanctioned by whom? Surely, not the leaders themselves. After all, legitimacy is something that is given, not taken.[187]

According to convention, leadership authority is sanctioned and thereby legitimized by our institutions: "The right to expect obedience inheres in the state or the institution of private property. The owners or government merely pass on this right to the manager."[188] Thus, formal leaders are supposedly legitimate because owners or shareholders or a Board of Trustees say they are. Little wonder so many leaders restrict their allegiances to the interests of these particular stakeholders. But in a *free* society, authority is legitimized by consent of the governed. And those being "governed" by organizations are those being "affected" by organizations. Thus, only the stakeholders can sanction leadership as legitimate, and this includes *all* of the stakeholders, not just a privileged few. So, the legitimacy of leadership is directly proportional to the range and number of stakeholders being served—*legitimate* leadership is *servant* leadership. As Robert K. Greenleaf wrote:

> A new moral principle is emerging which holds that the only authority deserving of one's allegiance is that which is freely given and knowingly granted...in response to, and in proportion to, the clearly evident servant nature of the leader. Those who choose to follow this principle will not casually accept the authority of existing institutions. Rather, they will freely respond only to individuals who are chosen as leaders because they are proven and trusted as servants.[189]

The chart on the facing page—*Legitimacy Criteria for Formal Leaders*—outlines and lists factors for evaluating the legitimacy of a leader or leadership group.

QUALIFICATIONS FOR LEADERS

What qualities and abilities do legitimate and effective leaders need to have? According to the research, most of us look for leaders to be honest, competent, forward-looking and inspiring.[192] Of these qualities, people rank honesty as the most important. How do we judge a leader's honesty?...Simple. We pay attention and watch what happens.

> Leaders are considered honest by their constituents when they do what they say they are going to do. Agreements not followed through, cover-ups, inconsistency between word and deed, are all indicators of a lack of honesty.[193]

Besides honesty, we look for leaders who are competent in their field, have a clear sense of direction, and are optimistic. These attributes make a leader *credible*, someone we can believe and have confidence in. This credibility has to be earned but is very fragile: it can be lost

LEGITIMACY CRITERIA FOR LEADERSHIP
A CHECKLIST FOR INDIVIDUALS & ORGANIZATIONS

INTENTIONS & MOTIVES

❑ The leader uses his or her position primarily to serve and enlarge the lives of others, rather than to personally acquire power, privilege, and material possessions.

MEANS & METHODS

❑ The leader practices moral symmetry, striving to balance the needs and well being of everyone affected.

❑ The leader uses participatory governance and processes to get things done, honoring basic human dignity and free will.

ENDS & OUTCOMES

❑ Those affected trust the leader. They know from personal experience that their well being is given appropriate consideration and weight in decision making.

❑ Those affected have the "experience of being served in a way that builds a society that is more just and loving and with greater opportunities for all."[190]

❑ Those served grow as persons. In being served, they "become healthier, wiser, freer, more autonomous, and more likely themselves to serve."[191]

with one thoughtless remark, inconsistent act, or broken agreement.[194] But credibility is not all of what is most essential for leadership. There is something much more. What is it?...*Care* and *concern* for those affected by the enterprise. As retired CEO and author Max DePree powerfully notes: "Leaders don't inflict pain; they bear pain... At the heart of being accountable is the matter of caring."[195] This caring includes the faculties of understanding, empathy, compassion, and love.

> The same issue is involved in being a corporation president, a physician, a teacher, a parent. Decisions affecting the lives of others must always be made. The best decision-makers are those who are willing to suffer the most over their decisions but still retain their ability to be decisive.[196]

People don't care how much you know until they know how much you care—about them. By combining credibility with caring, leaders are more than just believable or reliable: they are *trustworthy*. And this trustworthiness is the hallmark of legitimate leadership.

> Legitimacy begins with trust…The only sound basis for trust is for people to have the solid experience of being served…in a way that builds a society that is more just and more loving, and with greater opportunities for all…Trust is first.[197]

THE SPECTRUM OF LEADERSHIP

There are two basic but very different approaches to formal leadership: authoritarian and participatory. Authoritarian leaders emphasize *command* and *control*. They make the decisions (at least the most important ones) and then tell subordinates what to do. These leaders tend to focus on meeting the needs of particular stakeholders (usually the owners or shareholders), rather than balancing the needs of all the stakeholders. They also tend to view subordinates, employees, and the natural world instrumentally—as means to the ends of the organization. These leaders act as *bosses* who use the power of their position to support and sustain a privileged few at the expense of the many.

Participatory leaders, on the other hand, emphasize *service* and *the empowerment of others*. These leaders focus on understanding what is really going on and then laying the basis for collective, constructive action.[198] They thereby enable and empower others to co-create what is unfolding. Particapitory leaders do not use coercion or directives to get others to do things, nor do they use manipulation or other "artful" means. By sharing the power of their position with others, these leaders serve as "first among equals" and have "accountability without unilateral control." They are *servant leaders,* working on behalf of *all* the stakeholders.

> Research on successful leaders suggests a conception of effective leadership which emphasizes collective action and shared power rather than "command and control," and which requires a passionate commitment on the part of the "leader" to social justice…[T]he leadership model proposed here is designed to emphasize clarification of values, the development of self-awareness, trust, and the capacity to listen and serve others, and through collaborative work to bring about change for the common good.[199]

These two approaches to leadership—*boss* and *servant leader*—represent the opposite poles of a "spectrum of leadership" that we find in our workplaces, organizations and society. Individual leaders have profiles that place them somewhere on a continuum of possibilities between these extremes. The table on the following page outlines a comparison of these two distinct approaches. Assuming a world of polar opposites, for whom would you rather work—a boss or a servant leader?…For whom would you want your loved ones to work?…Why?…Which leader would you trust more?…Under which leader would you contribute most to the enterprise?…Which type of leadership do you think best contributes to creating a workable world?… If you are a formal leader yourself, where are *you* on *The Spectrum of Leadership*?

The Undiscussables

Some people claim that there is a "crisis in leadership," that good bosses are in short supply, and the ones we do have are often overstressed and burned out. Why is that?…Is there something inherent in being a boss that makes it especially challenging and difficult?… Workload?…Busyness?…External forces affecting the enterprise?… These are all probably contributing factors, but subordinates often work equally hard, are just as busy, and are also vulnerable to forces beyond their control. So we need to look elsewhere for answers, for

The Spectrum of Leadership
from Boss.............................to Servant Leader

GOVERNANCE

- Bosses take an authoritarian approach to governance and management. They make the important decisions.
- Bosses *exercise power over* others.

- Servant leaders use a participatory approach to governance and management. Important decisions are made by group process and consensus.
- Servant leaders *share power with* others.

ACCOUNTABILITY & CONTROL

- Bosses have accountability with unilateral control.
- Bosses "periodically judge the performance of each employee, controlling when, how, and even if performance reviews happen."[200]

- Servant leaders are "firsts among equals." They have accountability without unilateral control.
- "The servant leader asks to be coached and given honest feedback as well as offering the same to those served."[201]

GOALS & FOCUS

- Bosses focus primarily on meeting the needs of particular stakeholders.
- Bosses work to maintain existing authority and privilege.

- Servant leaders focus on balancing the legitimate needs of everyone affected.
- Servant leaders work to evoke and create a world that works for all.

VIEW OF OTHERS

- Bosses view subordinates as human resources (means to the ends of the organization).

- Servant leaders view others as partners and individual expressions of The Mystery (ends in themselves).

MEANING OF WORK

- Bosses view work as a transaction, whereby time and energy are exchanged for money.

- Servant leaders view work as a co-creative act of individuality and community.

something unique in the role and experience of bosses. And because these issues persist, we need to look at what we don't talk about—the "undiscussables" related to power—namely, *personal isolation* and *conflicts of interest*. Because we do not discuss these issues, they remain unresolved, undermining individuals in their roles as bosses and, in a larger sense, as human beings.

Personal Isolation Because bosses hold authoritarian power over others, they live in a fragmented, isolating world. Without a larger context of mutuality and trust, subordinates naturally shrink away and withhold from those to whom they are vulnerable. Thus, bosses are typically isolated from the correcting influence of the surrounding community. This enables negative aspects of their instinct and character to grow unchecked, undermining them personally and professionally. In addition, since subordinates ultimately lack meaningful influence and control, they do not accept "ownership" for the system nor its problems. And there is no end to the problems. After all, being alive means dealing with myriad problems.

> To live means to *cope*, to contend and keep level with all
> sorts of circumstances, many of them difficult. Difficult
> circumstances present *problems*, and it might be said that
> living means, above all else, dealing with problems.[202]

In the authoritarian system, bosses stand alone and responsible—isolated from others and overburdened with problems.

Conflict of Interest To make matters worse, there is an inherent conflict of interest for bosses (as for all leaders) in their roles. Their decisions and actions affect all of the organization's stakeholders—including themselves. This inherent conflict of interest is neither recognized nor declared, and shadows much of what bosses think and do. Even efforts to further "the bottom line" or "the company" are questionable and suspect as guises for self-interest. After all, bosses are typically well-rewarded for taking good care of owners and shareholders, often with little or no regard for other stakeholders.

These issues are rarely acknowledged, let alone addressed. So their energies play out unconsciously and unchecked, leaving bosses feeling overburdened, troubled, anxious, and lonely. Convention claims that bosses can find answers and relief through externals—the acquisition of new skills, techniques, and knowledge. But these ultimately fail in getting to the root of the troubles. That is because the basic issue that bosses have to contend with is not "out there" but "in here."

> You can pick up quick, easy techniques that may work in short-term situations. But secondary traits alone have no permanent worth. Eventually, if there isn't deep integrity and fundamental character strength, failure will replace short-term success.[203]

In the words of Harry Levinson: "To lead presupposes having much of one's own psychological house in order."[204] If we accept this premise and look within, we discover that we carry a good measure of self-interest and fear in our role as a boss. Our hidden agenda (what's in this for me) and internalized conflict (me versus others) cause us to be closed, strategic, indirect, and suspicious, separating us from others and arousing feelings of misgiving. As psychoanalyst Eric Fromm explained it:

> I am envious of those who have more and afraid of those who have less. But I have to repress these feelings in order to represent myself (to others as well as to myself) as the smiling, rational, sincere, kind human being everybody pretends to be.[205]

This self-interest and fear also lie at the heart of bureaucratic culture. When our primary focus is hanging on to what we already have or further climbing the organizational ladder, we become overly cautious and dependent.

> The bureaucratic belief is that we will move ahead in the organization by not making mistakes. The common feeling is that mistakes are punished much more vigorously

than achievements are rewarded…As we move up the organization, we become more concerned about what we have to lose than what we are trying to create.[206]

A LIFE CHOICE & JOURNEY

Once we understand how self-interest and fear relate to our difficulties, we can choose to do and experience something else. And here we have a *life choice* to make.

Do I embrace ambition, indulgence, and comfort through a career? Or do I pursue service without the promise of reward or proof that it will make a difference?…Do I see work as making a living, getting ahead, providing, and dying? Or do I see it as the chance to foster healing, hope, and the possibilities of life?[207]

This choice is between *having* and *being*, a choice that spiritual teachers and sages throughout history have made central to their systems.[208] And they consistently admonished us to free ourselves from "the spell of matter," claiming that if we made material acquisition, wealth, and parochial self-interest our paramount aim it would lead to disaster.[209] Choosing *to be* rather than *to have*, however, does not mean completely abandoning our self-interest, putting ourselves and our families at undue risk. Rather, it means extending our care and concern to everyone affected by what we decide and do. Once we choose to do that, we can begin our journey from boss to servant leader. Although each of our journeys will be different, reflecting who we are and the particular circumstances in which we live and work, there are two basic principles suggested by those who have gone before: speak the truth and operate from love.[210]

Speak the Truth This means being authentic and transparent. It includes staying in intimate contact with those around us (including subordinates), making our doubts, fears, misgivings, and limitations part of our dialogue with them.[211] It also includes creating openness and choice in organizational processes whenever we can, and speaking the truth to power (the bosses above us).

Operate from Love This means accepting people for who and what they are, and being committed to furthering their well-being and growth.

> This has little to do with emotions. It has everything to do with intentions—commitment to serve one another, and willingness to be vulnerable in the context of that service... [It is about] the full and unconditional commitment to another's *completion*, to another being all that she or he can and wants to be."[212]

With these two principles in mind, we can strive to live out and accomplish the high-leverage roles and ways of being for the practice of servant leadership, such as listed in the chart on the facing page, *Roles and Ways of Being—A Checklist for Servant Leaders.*

FROM LEADERSHIP TO FOLLOWERSHIP

What happens in an organization or workplace under servant leadership?...Plenty. Servant leadership evokes great *followership*. And while rarely mentioned, followers are as important as leaders. "Without followers, little gets done; with them, mountains get moved... Followers represent the bulk and substance of any enterprise."[216] Great followership, according to teacher and author Robert Kelly, has two dimensions.

> The first dimension is independent, critical thinking. The best followers are described as individuals who think for themselves, give constructive criticism, [and] are their own person...Yet independent thinking is only half of the followership equation. [There is] a second dimension: active engagement...The best followers take initiative, assume ownership, participate actively, [and] are self-starters.[217]

ROLES AND WAYS OF BEING
A CHECKLIST FOR SERVANT LEADERS[213]

STEWARD

Servant leaders hold the enterprise in trust for society, and are in service to everyone affected.

❑ **Governing Ideas.** Servant leaders focus on the *governing ideas* of the enterprise, including its purpose, values, and vision.[214] These ideas are about creating a workable and sustainable world. This brings meaning to the work and makes the enterprise worthy of our commitment and energy.

❑ **Alignment.** Servant leaders work to align the organization's mission, values, structure, systems, and processes, thereby creating an enterprise that has integrity and works synergistically.

❑ **Accountability.** Servant leaders hold themselves and the enterprise accountable to *all* the stakeholders. They assume responsibility for what does or does not happen, and they provide a reckoning on such.

ROLE MODEL

Servant leaders embody the ethics and behaviors desired of community members and others.

❑ **Trustworthiness.** Servant leaders are authentic, competent, and caring.

❑ **Sense of Adventure.** Servant leaders have accountability without unilateral control. And they put themselves at risk to do what is right.

❑ **Caring and Respect for Others.** Servant leaders genuinely care about and deeply respect others. They create systems in which people can share power and influence. They accept others, thereby supporting their authenticity.

❑ **Whole Person Approach.** Servant leaders make all of themselves available to the community—body, mind, and spirit; thoughts and feelings; strengths and weaknesses. They are transparent.

CHANGE AGENT

Servant leaders help to evoke and create a future that is desirable.

❑ **Framing Reality.** Servant leaders help people achieve more accurate, insightful, and empowering views of reality.

❑ **Generating Energy.** Servant leaders tell the truth about the current reality and hold a positive sense of possibility or vision of what could be. This creates tension and energy that help people move forward together.[215]

❑ **Creating a Domain for Participation.** Servant leaders share power, thereby creating a domain for others to co-create what is unfolding.

Servant leaders create a domain that evokes and nourishes independent critical thinking and active engagement by followers. In this shared space and field, leadership is no longer synonymous with hierarchical position. Rather, it is about the combined active engagement of the group.[218] The keys to this engagement are shared power and trust. Followers have the power to meaningfully influence and co-create what is unfolding, and they trust the formal leader and community that they can be authentic without fear of retribution. With these as context, all that is required are opportunities for meaningful engagement, which can occur in myriad ways — through meetings, dialogue sessions, planning sessions, e-mail, retreats, workshops, task groups, etc. Thus, servant leadership is *meta*leadership, whereby a culture and domain are created in which "the agents of leadership are abundant."[219] After all, in a given situation, most any follower can contribute as a leader and vice versa, depending on his or her unique gifts and the particular needs of the moment.

Changelessness is a sign of death,
transformation a sign of life.

~ Lama Govinda

We are always talking about changing
society...
but never about changing <u>who</u> is
responsible for it.

~ J. Krishnamurti

CHANGE & TRANSFORMATION

Change is defined as "the act or process of becoming different." Our universe and world are constantly changing: stars form and collapse, mountains rise and erode, glaciers come and go, civilizations rise and fall. We are each born, grow old, and will die. And throughout that time our bodies undergo continuous change. In fact, 600 billion cells of our body are dying and being regenerated every day—a mind-boggling 10 million cells per second. Interestingly, shamans and tribal healers see all of this change as nothing less than the *aliveness* of the Universe. As shaman Serge Kahli King explains:

> Life is not limited to plants, animals, and humans, because
> life is defined as movement. Some things move very slowly,
> like rocks, and some things move very quickly, like light.
> For the shaman these are simply different kinds of life.[220]

In modern civilization the rate of change itself is changing, increasing daily, along with its scale and impact. Thus, the nature and essence of our material reality and existence is a continual process and flow of things changing and becoming different. Nothing remains the same or endures: some changes are just slower than others. So, everything, including each one of us, is on its way to somewhere else.

CHANGE OR PERISH!

Historians have identified the inability to change and adapt as a major factor in the decline of civilizations. "When social structures and behavior patterns become so rigid that society can no longer adapt to changing situations…it will break down and eventually disintegrate."[221] At the personal level, our ability to change and adapt is a prerequisite for mental health and well-being. Clinging to set ways of perceiving and responding is the basis for much of our society's mental illness. Some claim that most psychotherapy patients have a sense of helplessness, and an inner conviction of being unable to change.[222] What is true for civilizations is apparently true for individuals: to stay alive and healthy, we must be willing and able to change and adapt. Researchers say this holds true for any *open system*—ones that exchange energy with their environment. This includes "systems" ranging from a chemical solution to a human being. In trying to identify the patterns common to successful change in open systems, Marjorie Kelly notes that:

> These self-renewing systems are resilient more than stable, maintaining themselves not through rigidity but adaptation...If an ability to break apart and reorganize is the mark of a resilient system, an inability to change is the mark of a decaying system.[223]

Still, while change is natural and necessary, it can also be difficult. After all, *change* (something becoming different) can differ from *progress* (something becoming better): while all progress is change, not all change is progress. In addition, we often experience the loss of old ways as painful. So even though we may agree that change is necessary, there is often a strong tendency to maintain the status quo. Referring to this paradox and dilemma, historian and teacher J. Bartlet Brebner wrote:

> Part of human nature resents change, loves equilibrium, while another part welcomes novelty, loves the excitement of disequilibrium. There is no formula for the resolution of this tug of war, but it is obvious that absolute surrender to either invites disaster.[224]

It is our capacity to change that empowers us to solve problems, take advantage of opportunities, grow, heal, and complete ourselves. Individuals, organizations, and societies, therefore, are competent to the extent that they are willing and able to adapt and change.

CHANGE IN THE WORKPLACE

Peter Drucker claimed that organizations need to be organized and managed for *constant* change and innovation.

> Society, community, and family are all conserving institutions. They try to maintain stability and to prevent, or at least slow, change. But the modern organization is a destabilizer. It must be organized for innovation...[and]

for the systematic abandonment of whatever is established, customary, familiar, and comfortable, whether that is a product, service, or process; a set of skills; human and social relationship; or the organization itself.[225]

These organizational changes and innovations can be symptomatic or systemic. *Symptomatic* changes, also called "quick fixes," do not change the basic nature of the system; they are extensions and extrapolations of what already exists. As such, they typically do not require much work, nor do they threaten the established order related to social power and privileges. Leaders understandably search for the quick-fix—reading the latest management books, attending seminars, listening to motivational speakers—in hopes of finding easy solutions to their workplace problems and dilemmas. But these approaches come and go while the nature of people's experience remains pretty much the same. *Systemic* changes, on the other hand, act on the underlying properties of an organization or workplace, thereby changing the nature of the system and experience. They are *transformational*, representing a discontinuity with the previous status quo.

Organizational theorists have espoused various models and strategies for organizational and workplace change and transformation. Early approaches outlined a staged process of *unfreezing* a system, *changing* it, and then *re-freezing* it. Social scientists later promoted *force-field* approaches, in which the forces supporting the change were reinforced and those opposing it were reduced. More recent approaches include envisioning a preferred future (e.g., What do we want to create?) and then working backwards.[226] The *creative tension* between "the vision of where we want to be" and "the truth of where we are now" then works to help pull the enterprise forward.

The Art of Enrollment

Most important or significant changes in organizations and workplaces require that people modify something about the way they think, feel, or behave. Author and speaker William Bridges, therefore, makes a distinction between *external changes* (in policies, practices or structure) and *internal transitions* (the psychological reorientation that people have to go through). From this perspective, people need to undergo three separate processes to integrate and accomplish change: (1) saying goodbye to the old, (2) coping through a "neutral zone" of uncertainty and not knowing, and then (3) moving forward in new ways.[227] But no one can really make another person change. "Each of us guards a gate of change that can be opened only from the inside."[228] Thus, the challenge for organizations and leaders is not merely to identify what changes are needed, but to do it in a way that builds and galvanizes support for the endeavor.

A prevailing theme in management circles is that employees generally resist change in the workplace. While this may be true, they often do so for sound reasons. Consider the following perspectives:

- In studying resistance to change, a central theme emerges. Change agents are invariably seen as people trying to impose their will on a group. No matter in what way change is advocated…resisters to change insist that change is being forced on them.[229]

- People resist being changed—especially when the change appears to have a payoff primarily for someone else.[230]

- The new story explains resistance not as fact of life, but as evidence of an act against life. Life is in motion, constantly creating, exploring, discovering. Newness is its desire. Nothing alive, including us, resists these creative motions. But all of life resists control. All of life pushes back against any process that inhibits its freedom to create itself.[231]

- Generally speaking, the person most comfortable with any particular change is the one proposing it. [And] if we looked at employees' lives as a whole, instead of at just their reaction to the iniative we're pushing, we might have considerable difficulty finding this widespread and generalized resistence to change.[232]

Much of the resistance employees have to change is evoked by where they live and work in an authoritarian system. In such systems a small, privileged group of individuals is typically involved in major decision-making and planning, while most everyone else affected or needed for implementation is unrepresented. This lack of involvement and participation is a significant source of employee resistance to change. And it is simply part of the natural dynamic of the "vulnerable versus the powerful"—the "have-nots versus the haves"— "us versus them." Research long ago identified a core principle for successful change: people are much more likely to support a change when they participate in the overall process. Those with a stake in the problem should help *both* to define it and to solve it. In the words of teacher and writer Stephen Covey: "Without involvement, there is no commitment. Mark it down, asterisk it, circle it. *No involvement, no commitment.*"[233] Experience and research has repeatedly demonstrated this simple truth. The following table includes this and other conditions that serve to foster employee support and enroll others for workplace change.

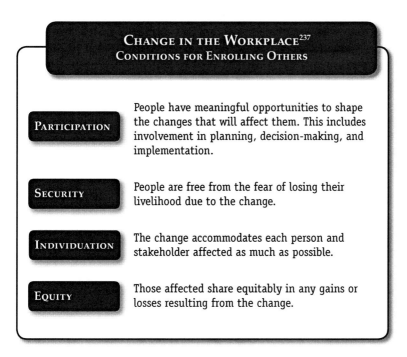

CHANGE IN THE WORKPLACE[237] **CONDITIONS FOR ENROLLING OTHERS**	
PARTICIPATION	People have meaningful opportunities to shape the changes that will affect them. This includes involvement in planning, decision-making, and implementation.
SECURITY	People are free from the fear of losing their livelihood due to the change.
INDIVIDUATION	The change accommodates each person and stakeholder affected as much as possible.
EQUITY	Those affected share equitably in any gains or losses resulting from the change.

PRINCIPLES FOR TRANSFORMATION _____

The Wisdom Traditions have long been interested in change and transformation. But, interestingly, their approaches differ markedly from those typically used by coventional management experts and organizational consultants. First and foremost, these traditions emphasize long-term effort and *being*, rather than short-term interventions and *doing*. Transformational change is viewed as a conscious journey for creating ourselves, rather than a reaction for coping with a changing world. The life challenges we face are viewed not so much as problems; rather, they are viewed as the raw material needed for catalyzing and sustaining the process and journey.

Since each person and situation is unique, what is most helpful is a set of *principles* that facilitates and guides the transformational process within the context of our different, everyday worlds. The Wisdom Traditions, therefore, all espouse principles for right living—the Eight-Limbed Path of Yoga, the Golden Rule, the Ten Commandments of Judaism and Christianity, the Eight-Fold Path of Buddhism, etc. These principles, based upon millennia of human experience, are value-based injunctions for intention and conduct. As such, they represent "ways of being." While they undoubtedly serve as standards to promote a just and workable world, their primary purpose is to facilitate personal change and transformation. According to these traditions, the process of deep change and transformation is simply the conscious application of a few basic principles to the moment-to-moment choices we make in our daily lives. As we strive and succeed in living out these principles, the journey increasingly becomes one with the destination.

Based on a study of the Wisdom Traditions, cultural anthropologist Angeles Arrien identified four universal principles that facilitate and support transformational change. According to Arrien, these principles have guided tribal leaders and change masters—including chiefs, medicine men and women, shamans, teachers, and seers—throughout time and across cultures.[235] This "Four-Fold Way" is outlined in the following chart.

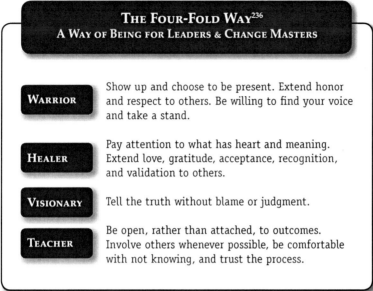

THE FOUR-FOLD WAY[236]
A WAY OF BEING FOR LEADERS & CHANGE MASTERS

WARRIOR	Show up and choose to be present. Extend honor and respect to others. Be willing to find your voice and take a stand.
HEALER	Pay attention to what has heart and meaning. Extend love, gratitude, acceptance, recognition, and validation to others.
VISIONARY	Tell the truth without blame or judgment.
TEACHER	Be open, rather than attached, to outcomes. Involve others whenever possible, be comfortable with not knowing, and trust the process.

Transformational principles have also been formulated for organizations and businesses, including the following:

- **Caux Round Table "Principles for Business."** The *Principles for Business* are based on the Western idea of *human dignity* and the Japanese concept of *kyosei*. The former relates to the sacredness and value of each person, while the latter relates to the concept of "living and working together for the common good, enabling cooperation and mutual prosperity to coexist with healthy and fair competition."[237]

- **Principles for Global Corporate Responsibility.** Developed by the Interfaith Center on Corporate Responsibility, these principles outline benchmarks for measuring business performance in the areas of human rights, just wages, working conditions, the environment, and sustainable community development.

Perhaps the simplest and most elegant system of principles for organizations was proposed by James O'Toole, a thought leader on business ethics. Based on a study of corporations that were both profitable and socially responsible, his system consists of four "Principles of Excellence" for the practice of organizational transformation. These principles—*moral symmetry, high purpose, high aim*, and *continuous learning*—are defined in the following table.[238]

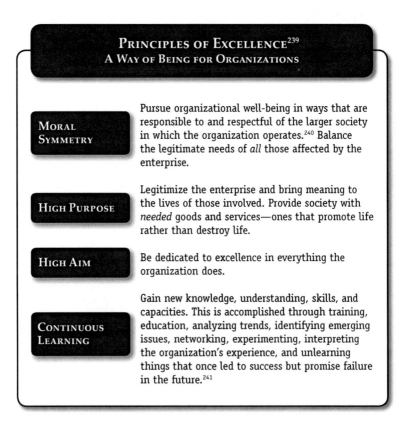

PRINCIPLES OF EXCELLENCE[239] A WAY OF BEING FOR ORGANIZATIONS	
MORAL SYMMETRY	Pursue organizational well-being in ways that are responsible to and respectful of the larger society in which the organization operates.[240] Balance the legitimate needs of *all* those affected by the enterprise.
HIGH PURPOSE	Legitimize the enterprise and bring meaning to the lives of those involved. Provide society with *needed* goods and services—ones that promote life rather than destroy life.
HIGH AIM	Be dedicated to excellence in everything the organization does.
CONTINUOUS LEARNING	Gain new knowledge, understanding, skills, and capacities. This is accomplished through training, education, analyzing trends, identifying emerging issues, networking, experimenting, interpreting the organization's experience, and unlearning things that once led to success but promise failure in the future.[241]

THE REST OF THE STORY

Specialized fields of study and an entire industry of experts and consultants are dedicated to the art and science of organizational development and workplace change. These professionals have been working with formal leaders over the last several decades to increase the effectiveness of our organizations and workplaces. But their legacy seems a modest one, at best. So what is going on? Why hasn't their work been more effective? In pondering these questions, consider the following injunctions from the Wisdom Traditions:

- As in everything else, I must start with myself.[242]

- I must first know myself.[243]

- The first thing you must do to improve others is improve yourself.[244]

- The only way to change the world is to change yourself.[245]

- Nothing happens without personal transformation.[246]

- Personal transformation is the first step in organizational transformation.[247]

- We want transformation through legislation, through outward revolution, through systems, but yet we are personally and inwardly untransformed.[248]

The Wisdom Traditions are clear on this: real change and transformation is an "inside-out" affair. That is, *organizational* change and transformation is preceded by *personal* change and transformation. As statesman and spiritual leader Mahatma Ghandi put it: "Be the change you wish to see in the world." More recently, this admonition was restated as, "Be the change the world needs."[249] These traditions are not talking about developing more skills for manipulating the external world; they are talking about something else. To better understand what this *something else* is, it is helpful to digress a bit.

Philosophers have long divided reality into three spheres or domains—the I, the We, and the It. Also known as *The Big Three*, they have consistently appeared in systems of thought throughout history and around the world. We also know them as: Self, Culture, and Nature...Art, Morality, and Science...Buddha, Sangha, and Dharma... the Beautiful, the Good and the True. We can map and divide our reality into these three realms, as shown in the following chart, based on the work of philosopher and writer Ken Wilber.[250]

THE BIG THREE[251]
DOMAINS OF REALITY

INTERIORS (CONSCIOUSNESS)

THE WORLD OF "I"
WHO AM I?
- self-awareness
- truthfulness
- intentions
- sincerity
- integrity

THE WORLD OF "WE"
WHAT IS FAIR AND JUST?
- justness
- rightness
- values
- ethics and morals
- mutual understanding
- culture and worldview

EXTERIORS (FORM)

THE WORLD OF "IT"
WHAT IS GOING ON?

Individuals
- individual behavior
- knowledge
- skills
- competence

Social Systems
- functional fit
- mission statement
- organizational structure
- organizational systems

The right-hand realm of "It" is the objective world of forms, which we can see and measure with our own senses or with instrumentation. It is the world of *exteriors*. The left-hand realms of "I" and "We" are the subjective worlds of consciousness, which we cannot measure but only interpret. It is the world of *interiors*. Now here's the point: the reason that the experts, consultants, and leaders in our organizations and workplaces achieve such modest results is that they focus almost *exclusively* on the right-hand world—the world of exteriors—the World of It. That is also why the nature of our subjective experience remains pretty much the same even though so many other things are changing. It's not that what our experts and leaders have been doing is wrong; rather, it is simply incomplete. In the words of Wilber: "There is nothing wrong with exteriors, they are just not the whole story."

| THE ZEN MONK

There was a Zen Roshi who approached a sidewalk vendor to buy lunch. After receiving his food and beverage, the monk handed over a fifty dollar bill. The vendor pocketed the large note and then went about taking care of the next customer. After waiting patiently for a few minutes, the monk spoke up and asked the vendor, "Excuse me, sir, but where is my change?" To which the vendor replied, "I'm sorry, Roshi, but I thought you knew—all change comes from within."

What do the sages and mystics mean when they talk about change and "seeking within"? They mean expanding our focus to include *interiors*—our interiors—the world of *consciousness*. More specifically, they mean developing our faculty of *self-awareness*.

> The power of the truth, seeing reality more and more as it is, cleansing the lens of perception, awakening from self-imposed distortions of reality—are different expressions of a common principle in almost all the world's great philosophic and religious systems. Buddhists strive to achieve the state of "pure observation," of seeing reality directly. Hindus speak of "witnessing," observing themselves and their lives with an attitude of spiritual detachment. The Koran ends with the phrase, "What a tragedy that man must die before he wakes up."[252]

What happens when we develop this faculty of self-awareness? Our level of consciousness changes. And these new or "higher" levels of consciousness (interiors) then become manifest in the world of form (exteriors), first in our behaviors and eventually in our social systems. *Thus, what we do and create in our workplaces and organizations is a manifestation of our level of consciousness.* As Czech President and playwright Vaclev Havel explained it to the U.S. Congress:

> Consciousness precedes being...the salvation of this human world lies nowhere else than in the human heart, in the human power to reflect, in human meekness, and in human responsibility. Without a global revolution in consciousness, nothing will change for the better in the sphere of our being as humans.[253]

THE INNER JOURNEY...AND "WAKING UP"

How do we go about developing our power of self-awareness and level of consciousness? Over millennia, the Wisdom Traditions have created and evolved different schools of practice and methods for doing such, including various combinations of sitting or moving meditation, prayer, dancing, drumming, fasting, extended sensory or social isolation, plant medicines, and shamanic journeying. These "technologies of the sacred" have been augmented by a wide range of contemporary modalities, including psychotherapy, breathwork, healing touch, and various forms of energy work. Generally, a mix of approaches is needed to address the various levels and dimensions of our human nature (e.g., physical, emotional, mental and spiritual). Fortunately, our own body/mind is the primary tool used for the work, something that is readily available to each of us.

When we follow the instructions of those who have gone before us and do the work over time, a remarkable process of self-discovery unfolds—an Inner Journey—that encompasses different types of awakenings.[254] These openings enable us to better see and apprehend the true nature of reality and of ourselves. They can unfold in series, one following the other, or concurrently over time. In rare instances, they can occur simultaneously in a sudden flash of insight and recognition. And they can happen to anyone, regardless of their chronological age or circumstances.

Awakening to Our Freedom The first type of awakening relates to our own suffering and to the possibility of freedom. Here, we develop a different sense of perspective on ourselves, thereby gaining some distance from the feelings and thoughts that naturally arise within us. From this "other place," we can see a lot. First and foremost, we can see how much of our suffering is caused by our own ignorant ways and thinking. This includes our cravings and obsessions, unconscious projections, self-criticism, guilt about the past, worries about the future, and the various stories we tell ourselves (e.g., "This line should be moving faster," "I'm not good enough," etc.). We can also see memories and unexpressed emotions that somehow remain incomplete, as well as aspects of ourselves that heretofore lived in shadow or darkness.

> This requires that we be willing to accept the totality of
> ourselves—including our sensual desires, self-doubts,
> anger, laziness, restlessness, fears, and so on. We cannot
> move beyond the habitual pushes and pulls of these forces
> until we are conscious of their presence in our lives.[255]

Such "sightings" lead to greater capacity to review and release aspects of ourselves that have somehow encumbered us from enjoying a more open and joyous approach to life. Eventually, we realize that this other place—*the witness*—is not just a different perspective on things, but actually a more essential part of ourselves than the accidental elements we have been noticing and looking at. By "accidental," I mean any aspect that was shaped and determined by the particulars of our life experience and domestication into family and society. Unlike these conditional aspects of being, the witness has always been with us, remains unchanged, and is already perfectly OK. Once we are grounded there, we discover or sense that it is a more profound and enduring, albeit ineffable, part of who or what we really are. From this witness place of unchanging OKness, we are better able to fully face and accept ourselves and what is.

We also become more inner-directed, adopting different ways of being and new life strategies. Rather than focusing on accumulating conventional commodities, such as wealth, fame or power, we focus on having the fullest possible experience of life in the present moment. We realize that we are not helpless victims having a life experience, but creators of the experience itself. And so, we learn to *respond* to life rather than *react* to it; consciously choosing what we do as a creative act in manifesting ourselves and in creating our world. Through these kinds of awakenings, we put our psychological house in order and learn to say "yes" to all of life, with a sense of presence, gratitude and freedom.

Awakening to Our Connectedness The second type of awakening relates to our *connectedness*. For many of us, it follows naturally from the first: as we come to accept ourselves, so, too, do we come to accept others. This acceptance—or love—radiates naturally outward from ourselves to others. It is a bridge of connection and empathy, across which we feel the pain and suffering of others. While their pain and suffering looks different from our pain and suffering, we realize that it is essentially the same: it is the pain and suffering of a living, aware being. Thus, our circle of care and compassion expands. "This does not mean that we stop caring for ourselves, only that we include more and more others for whom we also evidence a genuine concern and compassion."[256] While some people tend to emphasize care and relationship, others tend to emphasize rights and justice. Still, the underlying theme is the same: extending what we want for ourselves and our loved ones to others.[257]

As the process matures, the sense of who or what we are continues to change. Even though we still identify with our skin-encapsulated organism, we also experience a growing sense of identity with our awareness and the rest of creation. Where does all this end? According to the mystics, from saints to physicists, East and West, we eventually "wake up" to discover that, somehow or someway, we are intimately connected and one with all that is.

> Mystical experience is, simply, a transcendence of our
> normal state of consciousness in which we believe ourselves
> to be separate individuals into a consciousness of the
> oneness of all life, sentient and insentient, huge as a galaxy
> and tiny as a quark.[258]

Through these kinds of awakenings, we realize that we are not only life*forms* that inhabit an immense and seemingly threatening universe, but also life*streams* that are part of a vast, cosmic ocean of being. Our bodies, which we typically sense as more or less solid, are revealed to be rivers of matter and energy, flowing out of and back into the world around us. The separate mind/body "thing" that we thought we were — a constellation of images and roles that represent our normal sense of self-identity — now seems to be an artificial construct imposed upon a mystery. We see that we are both beings and *inter*beings, living in a universe that has two realities: conventional reality, in which there are separate objects and entities that have names and defined relationships, where you are you and I am me; and another reality, in which there are no separate entities, where there is only a single field and continuum of interrelated life, energy and matter.[259] Interestingly, since there are no "things" in this other reality, there is no birth or death either. This sense of connectedness, therefore, is a powerful antidote to the fear of death that shapes and underpins conventional life strategies. As one seeker put it:

> I did not merely come to believe, but I saw that the
> universe is not composed of dead matter, but is, on the
> other hand, a living Presence; I became conscious in myself
> of eternal life.[260]

But the Inner Journey is no "picnic in the park." Indeed, it can be harrowing. Profound grief can arise when we actually see how much of our life has been inauthentic or wasted. And existential terror can flare up when we cut through conventional illusions of self identity. The fact is, awakenings into higher levels of consciousness can expose and threaten our existing life strategies, which encompass things like relationships, marriages, and careers. So there are road bumps on the path that can evoke extraordinarily difficult periods for us, what the mystics call "dark nights of the soul."

In addition, awakenings usually are not integrated at first; rather, they are "temporarily realized." Because our mind/body systems are hard-wired for survival and separateness, the mind and ego are always generating a steady stream of countervailing thoughts and feelings. The society we live in and most of the people around us are doing likewise. For these and other reasons, even after awakening to more insightful and powerful understandings of reality, we tend to fall back into habituated patterns of thinking and living. But through the power of the sacred technologies and awareness, we can awaken, again…and again…and again. Over time, we are able to integrate and stabilize these experiences into a higher level of consciousness and new ways of being.

And so, through our own good fortune, grace and/or sacred technologies, we can journey from *egocentric* to *ethnocentric* to *worldcentric*. Even though the places we inhabit and routes we take are unique, the destination is the same. Our common calling is to identify with and care for all—ourselves, our loved ones, our neighbors, our tribe, other tribes, other peoples, future generations, other life forms, living systems, and even creation itself. At the most basic level, becoming fully human is about growing into this larger embrace. When we are able to do so, the world is no longer a problem with which we cope, but a mystery for which we care.[261] Importantly, even if we have been enjoying comfort and material gain under the established order, we become willing to change that order to further a world that works for all. This makes deep non-violent change truly possible in both our workplaces and greater society. Referring to seekers in a different context, but applicable to most anyone awakening into higher levels of consciousness, Stanislav Grof put it this way:

> [These] individuals…tend to develop a sense of planetary
> citizenship, reverence for life, deep ecological sensitivity,
> spirituality of a universal and all-encompassing type,
> aversion to violence, and reluctance to view aggression as
> an acceptable form of conflict resolution. Such radical inner

transformation and rise to a new level of consciousness might be humanity's only real chance for survival.[262]

ACKNOWLEDGEMENTS ⎯⎯⎯⎯⎯⎯⎯⎯⎯⎯⎯⎯⎯

This guide was made possible by the teachers, mentors, family, friends, colleagues, and other special people who graced my life either directly or indirectly. Foremost among them are the following.

Teachers & Mentors Barb Brodsky and Aaron, my spiritual teachers, who wisely and gently admonished me over a decade ago to "heal thyself" before writing this book, and then guided and supported me on that journey. Bill Bottum, my mentor, friend, and the very first "first among equals." Carl Christoff, my best friend, shaman, and Dharma brother, who helped me discover and live out who I truly am. Alex and Michael, my sons, who are teaching me about freedom. Bernie and Dorothy Ann Coyne, who welcomed me into their household at Sunnyside as an "elder in training."

Colleagues at Work Roy Christian, Ken Davis, Ricky Hoover, Vicky Hueter, Joe Kennedy, and Jeff Schroeder, and the rest of the gang in the Housing facilities department at U of M who joined me in living out these ideas in the workplace. Bernadette Malinoski, (Workplace Partners, L.L.C.), who invariably found "the light in the dark" and facilitated much of what was created. Barb Cecil (Ashland Institute), who led us through dialogue into deeper community. Anita Zimmerman and John DeSouza (Interax, Inc.), who got us "out of the blocks," and who contributed their process wisdom and fearlessness to some of the most challenging parts of the journey. Larry Spears and staff of the Robert K. Greenleaf Center for Servant Leadership and its affiliate community, who recognized and legitimized our work when most everyone else thought we were crazy. University of Michigan executive administrators, who genuinely supported us in creating an alternative governance system in the workplace.

Family & Friends Jack Christ, Ginny Gilmore, Sharon Hacker, Brenda Herman, Kris Kurnit, Frank and Larissa, Armando Lopez, Hal Rothbart, Sandy Wiener, Marie Woodrich, and Cathy Wolfe, who encouraged and supported the work. Roann Altman (Communicate for Success) and Dorothy Lenz, who edited the manuscript. Laura SanFacon, who saved me from a life I cannot describe without incriminating myself. Pumkin and Trish, who taught me about unconditional love and acceptance.

Other Special People Ken Wilber, whose work influenced many of the ideas herein. Peter Block, whose writings helped push me over the edge. Robert K. Greenleaf, who provided the language for what we were trying to live out. Stanislav Grof, whose work shaped so much of my journey and development. And all the other writers, authors, and teachers referenced herein, who helped clarify and affirm what my heart knew but my mind could not express.

Introduction

1 Peter Senge, *Business Ethics* interview, March/April 1993, 18.

2 Robert K. Greenleaf.

3 Wayne Muller, *Sabbath* (New York: Bantam Books, 1999), 11.

4 For more information, visit the University of Michigan's Web site at www.housing.umich.edu. Check out the *Facilities Council Handbook*

People

5 Peter Matthiessen, *The Snow Leopard* (New York: Viking Press, 1978), 232.

6 Douglass Adams, *The Hitchhiker's Guide to the Galaxy* (New York: Ballantine, 1980), 6.

7 Source unknown.

8 J. Samuel Bois, *The Art of Awareness*, 3rd edition (Dubuque: William C. Brown, 1978), 32.

9 Deepak Chopra.

10 Ken Carey, *Return of the Bird Tribes* (Kansas City: Uni-Sun, 1988), 27.

11 Arjuna Nick Ardagh, *Relaxing Into Clear Seeing* (Nevada City: SelfXPress, 1999), 22.

12 *Webster's New World Dictionary*, 2nd College edition. (The World Publishing Company, 1978).

13 *Webster's*.

14 George Leonard, *Adventures in Monogamy* (Los Angeles: Jeremy P. Tarcher), 89.

15 Angeles Arrien, *The Four-Fold Way* (San Francisco: Harper Collins, 1993), 79-80.

16 Geoff Carr, "The Proper Study of Mankind," *The Economist*, December 24th 2005-January 6th 2006, 4.

17 Martin Luther King, as quoted in address by University of Michigan Regent Nellie Varner.

18 Ervin Laszlo, *Science and the Akashic Field* (Rochester: Inner Traditions, 2004), 5-6.

19 Jack Hawley, *Reawakening the Spirit in Work: The Power of Dharmic Management* (Berrett-Koehler, 1993), 13.

20   George Leonard, 40.

21   *The American Heritage College Dictionary*, Third edition (Boston, Houghton Mifflin Company, Boston, 1997).

22   Roger Walsh, *Essential Sprituality* (New York: John Wiley & Sons, Inc., 1999), 24.

23   Ken Wilber, *A Brief History of Everything* (Boston: Shambhala Publications, 1996), 139.

24   Roger Walsh, 25.

25   Ken Wilber.

26   Ken Wilber, 261.

27   Stephen Levine, *Who Dies?* (New York: Doubleday, 1982), 1.

28   Duane Elgin, *Voluntary Simplicity* (New York: William Morrow, 1993), 121.

29   Ram Dass, *The Only Dance There Is* (Anchor Books, Garden City, 1974), 147.

30   Stanislav Grof. *The Adventure of Self-Discovery* (State University of New York Press, 1988), 265.

31   Roger Walsh, 7.

32   Peter Vaill, "Process Wisdom for a New Age," in *Transforming Work*, Ed. John Adams (Englewood Cliffs: Prentice-Hall, 1984), 31.

33   Geoff Carr, "The Proper Study of Mankind," *The Economist*, December 24, 2005-January 6, 2006, 11.

34   Sharif Abdullah, *Creating a World that Works for All* (Berrett-Koehler, 1999), 47-48.

35   *United Nations, Universal Declaration of Human Rights*, United Nations General Assembly: 2nd Session, December 10, 1988, Doc. A/811.

36   Donela Meadows. "What to Do as a Global Citizen," *Co-Op America Quarterly*, Summer 1992, 19.

37   Joseph Campbell. As quoted in interview by Bill Moyers, "Myth in Our Lives," *Utne Reader*, September/October 1988, 92.

38   David Meyers, *The Pursuit of Happiness* (New York: Avon, 1992), 34.

39   Eric Hoffer.

40   William Glasser, *The Control Theory Manager* (New York: Harper Business, 1994), 53-54.

41   Connirae Andreas, *Core Transformation: Reaching the Wellspring Within* (Moab: Real People Press, 1994), 19-20.

42 Connirae Andreas, 21-24.

43 Source unknown.

44 Sharif Abdullah, *Creating a World that Works for All* (Berrett-Koehler, 1999), 19-20.

WORK

45 *Webster's.*

46 Sam Keen, "Work and Worth," in *Mindfulness and Meaningful Work: Explorations in Right Livelihood,* Ed. Claude Whitmyer (Berkely: Parallax Press, 1994), 186-202.

47 *Webster's.*

48 *Webster's.*

49 As quoted by Rick Fields, with Peggy Taylor, Rex Weyler, and Rick Ingrasci, *Chop Wood, Carry Water* (Los Angeles: Jeremy P. Tarcher, 1984), 105.

50 Edmond Szekely, *Creative Work* (Cartago: International Biogenic Society, 1973), 17.

51 John Lobell, *The Little Green Book* (Boulder: Shambhala, 1982), 143.

52 Linda Naiman.,"Creativity and the Meaning of Work," *Perspectives on Business and Global Change,* 1998, Vol. 12. No. 1, 84.

53 E. F. Schumacher, "Good Work," in *Mindfulness and Meaningful Work: Explorations in Right Livelihood,* Ed. Claude Whitmyer (Berkeley: Parallax Press, 1994), 131.

54 Arnold Toynbee.

55 Source unknown.

56 Thomas Moore, "The Soul of Work," *Business Ethics,* March/April 1993, 7.

57 Peter Senge, *The Fifth Discipline: The Art and Practice of the Learning Organization* (New York: Doubleday, 1990), 307.

58 Edmond Szekely, *Creative Work* (Cartago: International Biogenic Society, 1973), 19.

59 Edmond Szekely, 18.

60 Tarthang Tulku, "Skillful Means," in *Mindfulness and Meaningful Work: Explorations in Right Livelihood,* Ed. Claude Whitmyer (Berkeley: Parallax Press, 1994), 28.

61 Kahlil Gibran, *The Prophet.*

62 Joel Henning, "I Make Beautiful: On Being Worthy of the Work We Do," *At Work,* November/December 1997, 22.

63 Source unknown.

64 Joan D. Chittiser, "How Shall We Live?" *Spirituality and Health,* December 2003, 31.

65 Edmond Szekely, 16.

66 Claude Whitmyer, "Doing Well and Doing Good" in *Mindfulness and Meaningful Work: Explorations in Right Livelihood,* Ed. Claude Whitmyer (Berkeley: Parallax Press, 1994), 15.

67 Lina Naiman, "Creativity and the Meaning of Work," *Perspectives on Business and Global Change,* Vol. 12 No. 1, 1998, 84.

68 United Nations, *Universal Delcaration of Human Rights,* U-N General Assembly: 2nd Session, December 10, 1948, Doc. A/811.

69 William J. O'Brien, *The Soul of Corporate Leadership* (Waltham: Pegasus Communications, 1998), 2.

70 Rick Fields, with Peggy Taylor, Rex Weyler, and Rick Ingrasci, *Chop Wood, Carry Water* (Los Angeles: Jeremy P. Tarcher, 1984), 109.

71 Edmond Szekely, 13.

72 Ram Dass and Paul Gorman, *How Can I Help?* (New York: Alfred A Knop, 1987), xi-xii.

73 Karl Albrecht and Ron Zemke, *Service America!* (Homewood: Dow Jones-Irwin, 1985), 36.

74 Chip Bell and Ron Zemke, "The Performing Art of Service Management" *Management Review,* July 1990.

75 Karl Albrecht and Ron Zemke.

76 Fritjof Capra. *The Turning Point* (New York: Bantam Books, 1983).

77 *The American College Dictionary.*

78 Fritjof Capra, 232.

79 Gerald Jampolsky, *Love Is Letting Go of Fear* (Berkeley: Celestial Arts, 1979), 53.

80 John Tosh, "The Secret of Good Customer Service? Good Employee Relations!" Address given at American Management Association Conference in Chicago, April 20, 1989.

81 Karl Albrecht and Ron Zemke, 39.

82 Based on the work of Karl Albrecht and Ron Zemke, 39-42.

83   Karl Albrecht and Ron Zemke, 96.

84   Arthur J. Deikman, "The Spiritual Heart of Service." Paper presented at Fetzner Institute Conference "Recovering the Spiritual Heart of Service," May, 1997.

85   Hugh Prother, *Notes to Myself.*

86   Remen, Rachel Naomi, "Helping, Fixing or Serving?" *Shambhala Sun*, September 1999, 25.

87   *Webster's New World Dictionary.*

88   Peter Drucker, *Management: Tasks, Responsibilities, Practices* (New York: Harper & Row, 1986), 3.

89   Jeremy Rifkin, "Work," *Utne Reader*, May-June 1995, 59.

90   Peter Drucker, "The New Pluralism," *Leader to Leader*, Fall 1999, 21.

91   Ralph Estes and Subashini Ganesan, "The Stakeholder Alliance: A New Bottom Line," *Perspectives on Business and Global Change*, Vol. 11 No. 4.

92   James O'Toole, *Vanguard Management* (New York: Berkeley Publishing Group, 1987), xvii.

93   Russ Ackoff. As quoted by Peter Senge in *Business Ethics*, March/April 1993, 17.

94   James Cayne, as quoted in *The New Leaders*, September/October 1992, 3.

95   Peter Koenig, "To Be 'Values Driven' Means Escaping the Profitability Trap," *At Work*, July/August 1997, 13.

96   Peter Drucker. As quoted in "The Man Who Invented Management," *New York Times Book Review*, January 11 1998, 5.

97   Peter Koenig, 12.

98   Paul Ciefuegos, "On Changing Corporate Charters," *At Work* September/October 1997.

99   Marjorie Kelly, "Maximizing Shareholders' Returns: A Legitimate Mandate?" *Perspectives on Business and Global Change*, Vol. 14 No. 1, 2000, 49.

100   Marjorie Kelly, 52.

101   Marjorie Kelly, 52.

102   Excerpt from publisher's promotional material for *The Great Awakening*, by David Loy.

103   Peter Koenig, 12-13.

104   John Elkington, *Cannibals with Forks* (New Society Publishers, 1998).

[105] Peter Senge. As quoted in *Business Ethics*, March/April 1993, 18.

[106] Based on the work of John Rawls, as developed by John Foley in *Driving Out Fear* (Los Alamos Ethics Training and Consulting, 1996), 34.

[107] Adapted from John Foley, 34.

[108] Kenneth Blanchard and Norman Vincent Peale, *The Power of Ethical Management* (New York: William Morrow and Company, 1988), 27.

[109] Barb Coffman, as quoted in workshop conducted at University of Michigan, February, 1998.

[110] William Isaacs, "Taking Fight: Dialogue, Collective Thinking, and Organizational Learning," *Organizational Dynamics* (American Management Association, 1993), 5.

[111] Peter Senge, 241.

[112] Marvin Weisbord and Sandra Janoff, *Future Search* (Berrett-Koehler, 1995), 5.

[113] Harrison Owen, *Open Space Technology* (Berrett-Koehler, 1997), 15.

[114] Juanita Brown and David Isaacas, *The World Café*.

Governance and Management

[115] *The American College Dictionary*, 3rd edition (Houghton Mifflin Company, 1993).

[116] Patricia McLagan and Christo Nel, *The Age of Participation* (San Francisco: Berrett-Koehler, 1995), 1.

[117] Patricia McLagan and Christo Nel, 18-19.

[118] Patricia McLagan and Christo Nel, 20.

[119] Patricia McLagan and Christo Nel, 15.

[120] Bertrand Russell.

[121] R. D. Laing.

[122] Clay Carr, "Managing Self-Managed Workers."

[123] William Glasser, 61-62.

[124] Larraine R. Matusak, "Power."

[125] James Surowiecki, "Overcompensating," *The New Yorker,* February 13 & 20, 2006, 54.

[126] William Glasser, *The Control Theory Manager* (Harper Business, 1994), 10.

[127] Richard Sennett, *Authority* (New York: Alfred A. Knopf, 1980).

[128] Trudy Heller, "Authority: Changing Patterns, Changing Times," in *Transforming Work*, Ed. John Adams (Alexandria: Miles River Press, 1984), 90.

[129] William J. O'Brien, *The Soul of Corporate Leadership*, (Waltham: Pegasus Communications, 1998), 4.

[130] Robert Greenleaf. *The Institution as Servant*, 13.

[131] Rensis Likert, *New Patterns of Management* (New York: McGraw-Hill, 1961), 116.

[132] Based on the work of Barry Oshry. See Barry Oshry, *Seeing Systems: Unlocking the Mysteries of Organizational Life* (San Francisco: Berrett-Koehler Publishers, Inc., 1995).

[133] William Glasser, 12.

[134] Sam Keen, "Work and Worth" in *Mindfulness and Meaningful Work: Explorations in Right Livlihoood*, Ed. Claude Whitmyer (Berkeley: Parallax Press, 1994), 186-202.

[135] Joseph Massie. *The Essentials of Management*, 3rd edition (Englewood Cliffs, New Jersey: Prentice Hall, 1979), 4.

[136] John Simmons and William Mares, *Working Together: Employee Participation in Action* (New York: New York University Press, 1985), 16.

[137] Edward E. Lawler III, *High Involvement Management* (SanFrancisco: Jossey-Bass, 1987), 42-43.

[138] David G. Bowers, *Systems of Organization* (Ann Arbor: University of Michigan Press, 1977), 3.

[139] Jon R. Katzenbach and Douglas K. Smith, *The Wisdom of Teams* (New York: Harper Business, 1994), 47-48.

[140] David G. Bowers, 52-54.

[141] Peter Block. Remarks in keynote address at 1994 International Conference on Servant Leadership. As quoted in *Servant Leader*, Fall 1994, 1.

[142] David Bowers.

[143] "A Survey of the Company," The Economist, January 21, 2006, 5.

[144] John Nienberg, "Creating Workplace Communities," *World Business Academy Perspectives*, Vol. 8 No. 1 1994, 42.

[145] University of Michigan Housing Facilities Department, *Facilities Council Handbook* (Ann Arbor: University of Michigan, 2000), 73.

146 Housing Facilities Department, 73.

147 Paula Underwood, *Sacred Among Her People* (A Tribe of Two, 1993).

148 Patricia McLagan and Christo Nel, "The Shift to Participation," *Perspectives on Business and Global Change*, Vol. 10 No. 1, 1996, 56.

149 Robert Kenny, "Spread Leadership," *Yes! A Journal of Positive Futures*, Fall 1999, 39.

150 Kenneth R. Hey and Peter D. Moore, "What the Caterpillar Doesn't Know," *Perspectives on Business and Global Change*, Vol. 12 No. 4, 33.

151 William J. O'Brien, 9.

152 Robert K. Greenleaf, *The Insitution as Servant* (Robert K. Greenleaf Center, 1972), 11.

153 Peter Block, *Stewardship* (Berrett-Koehler Publishers, 1993), xx.

154 Patricia McLagan and Christo Nel, 25

155 Barbara Shipka, "Relieving Spiritual Poverty in Our Organizations," *World Business Academy Perspectives*, Vol. 7, No. 3, 1999.

156 William J. O'Brien, 8.

157 *Business Week*, "Want to Boost Productivity? Try Giving Workers a Say," April 17, 1989.

158 Institute for Research on Learning, "IRL's Seven Principles of Learning: Challenging Fundamental Assumptions," 21st Century Learning Initiative, 1996, 3.

159 Patricia McLagan and Christo Nel, 27.

160 David G. Bowers, 22-23.

161 As quoted by Vinit Allen and Deborah Havland, "Reviving the Spirit of Community," *Catalyst*, September 1991, 20.

162 Lietaer. As quoted in *Inner Edge* June/July 1999.

163 Paula Underwood, *The Great Hoop of life* (Tribe of Two Press, 2000), 30-34.

164 Juanita Brown. As quoted in "Creating Community at Work," 2.

165 Kenneth R. Hey and Peter D. Moore, "What the Caterpillar Doesn't Know," *Perspectives on Business and Global Change*, Vol. 12 No. 4, 30.

166 Kenneth R. Hey and Peter D. Moore, 33.

167 John Nirenberg, "Creating Workplace Communities," *World Business Academy Perspectives*, Vol. 8 No. 1, 1994, 40-42.

LEADERS AND LEADERSHIP _____

[168]   *The American College Dictionary.*

[169]   Peter Drucker, *Management: Tasks, Responsibilities, Practices* (New York: Harper & Row, 1973), 6.

[170]   Peter Drucker.

[171]   Peter Drucker.

[172]   Donella H. Meadows, 49.

[173]   Paul Hawken, as quoted in *INC.*, April 1992.

[174]   Confucius.

[175]   John Heider, *The Tao of Leadership* (Atlanta: Humanics New Age, 1985), 13.

[176]   Stephen Covey, *The 7 Habits of Highly Effective People* (New York: Simon & Schuster, 1989), 217.

[177]   Lao-Tzu.

[178]   Max DePree, 1.

[179]   Harlan Cleveland, "Control: The Twilight of Hierarchy," *New Management*, 1985, 21.

[180]   Warren Bennis and Burt Nanus, *Leaders* (New York: Harper & Row, 1985), 221-226.

[181]   Robert K. Grenleaf, *The Servant as Leader* (Robert K. Greenleaf Center, 1970), 2.

[182]   Max DePree, 136.

[183]   Joseph Jaworksi, "Creating the Future," *The New Leaders*, September/October 1996, 5.

[184]   John Heider, 79.

[185]   Vaclev Havel, *Summer Meditations* (New York: Alfred A. Knopf, 1992), 8.

[186]   Parker J. Palmer, "Leading from Within: Reflections on Spirituality and Leadership." Address given in March 1990 (Washington, DC: The Servant Leadership School), 7.

[187]   John Renesch, "Legitimacy: The Power We Give Others," *The New Leaders*, January/February 1996, 7.

[188]   Jay Gailbraith, *Organization Design* (Reading, Massachusetts: Addison-Wesley, 1977), 15.

[189]   Robert K. Greenleaf, *The Servant Leader*, 4.

[190] Robert K. Greenleaf, *The Institution as Servant*, 19.

[191] Robert K. Greenleaf, *The Servant Leader*, 7.

[192] James Kouzes and Barry Posner, "The Credibility Factor: What Followers Expect from Their Leaders," *Management Review,* January 1990, 30.

[193] James Kouzes and Barry Posner, 30.

[194] James Kouzes and Barry Posner, 32.

[195] Max DePree, 36.

[196] M. Scott Peck, *The Road Less Travelled* (New York: Simon & Schuster, 1978), 76.

[197] Robert K. Greenleaf, *The Institution as Servant*, 19.

[198] Noam Chomsky. As quoted in "The Chomsky Tapes, I," *Z Magazine*, October 1995, 26.

[199] *NASPA Forum*, "Collaborative Approaches for Responsible Change," June/July 1995.

[200] Ann McGee-Cooper, "Accountability as Covenant: The Taproot of Servant-Leadership," *Insights on Leadership*, Ed. Larry Spears (New York: John Wiley & Sons, 1998), 78.

[201] Ann McGee-Cooper, 78.

[202] E. F. Schumacher, *A Guide for the Perplexed* (New York: Harper & Row, 1977), 120.

[203] Steven Covey, 22.

[204] Harry Levinson, *The Exceptional Executive* (Cambridge: Harvard University Press, 1968), 292.

[205] Erich Fromm, *To Have Or To Be?* (New York: Harper & Row, 1976), xxviii.

[206] Peter Block, *The Empowered Manager* (SanFrancisco: Jossey-Bass, 1987), 37.

[207] Joel Henning, "I Make Beautiful: On Being Worthy of the Work We Do," *At Work*, November/December 1997.

[208] Erich Fromm, 3.

[209] Ken Carey, 16.

[210] Donella Meadows, "What to Do as a Global Citizen," *Co-Op America Quarterly*, Summer 1992, 19.

[211] Peter Block, 43.

[212] Peter Senge, 285.

[213] The model presented here, emphasizing the roles of *steward*, *role model*, and *change agent*, is based on the work of Warren Bennis and Bert Nanus from their book *Leaders*.

[214] Peter Senge, 223-225.

[215] Peter Senge, 150-155.

[216] Robert Kelly, *The Power of Followership* (New York: Doubleday, 1991), quote from jacket cover.

[217] Robert E. Kelly, 93-94.

[218] Kathleen E. Allan, "Leadership as an Emergent Property of Individual and Group Interactions," *Inner Edge* October/November 2000, 21.

[219] Katrhleen E. Allen, 21.

CHANGE AND TRANSFORMATION

[220] Serge Kahli King, *Urban Shaman* (New York: Fireside,1990), 71.

[221] Fritjof Capra, *The Turning Point* (New York: Bantam Books, 1983), 28.

[222] M. Scott Peck, *The Road Less Traveled* (New York: Simon & Schuster, 1978), 43-44.

[223] Marjorie Kelly, "Taming the Demons of Change" *Business Ethics*, July/August 1993, 6.

[224] J. Bartlet Brebner.

[225] Peter Drucker, "The New Society of Organizations," *Harvard Business Review*, September-October 1992, 96-97.

[226] Peter Senge, 206.

[227] William Bridges and Susan Mitchell, "Leading Transiton: A New Model for Change," *Leader to Leader*, No. 16, Spring 2000.

[228] Marilyn Ferguson. As quoted in *The 7 Habits of Highly Effective People*, 60-61.

[229] James O'Toole, "Leading Change," as summarized in *Executive Book Summaries*, Soundview Vol. 17 No. 5, 8.

[230] Clay Carr, 55.

[231] Margaret J. Wheatley, "The New Story Is Ours to Tell," *Perspectives on Business and Global Change*.

[232] Clay Carr, 55.

233   Stephen Covey, *The 7 Habits of Highly Effective People* (New York: Simon & Schuster, 1989), 143.

234   Based on the work of Michael Macoby and Neal Herrick.

235   Angeles Arrien, *The Four-Fold Way* (SanFrancisco: Harper Collins, 1993), 7-8.

236   Angeles Arrien.

237   Cindy Mitlo, "A Matter of Principles" *Co-op America Quarterly*, Number 30, Spring 1996, 18.

238   James O'Toole, xvii-xix.

239   Based on the work of James O'Toole.

240   David Korten, "The End of Cowboy Capitalism," *At Work*, May/June 1999, 6.

241   Warren Bennis and Burt Nanus, *Leaders* (New York: Harper & Row, 1985), 194-203.

242   Vaclav Havel, in address given to U.S. Congress, 1990.

243   Socrates.

244   Taoist Aphorism.

245   Susana Barciela, "Dharmasala Dreaming: A Traveler's Search for the Meaning of Work" in *Insights on Leadership,* Ed. Larry Spears (John Wiley & Sons, 1998), 105.

246   W. Edwards Deming. As quoted in *Systems Thinker*, Volume 5, Number 9, November 1994,1.

247   Hey and Moore, 33.

248   Krishnamurti.

249   Don Beck. *Spiral Dynamics Integral* (Boulder: Sounds True, 2006)

250   Ken Wilber's *A Brief History of Everything* and *Sex, Ecology, and Spirituality*.

251   Adapted from the work of Ken Wilber.

252   Peter Senge, 161.

253   Vaclev Havel.

254   Joel and Michelle Levey, *The Fine Arts of Relaxation, Concentration, and Meditation*, (Somerville: Wisdom Publications, 2003), 85.

255   Duane Elgin, 132-133.

256   Ken Wilber, *A Theory of Everything*, 18.

257   Ken Wilber, *A Brief History of Everything*, 261.

[258] Robert Rabbin. "Spiritual Awakening in the Boardroom."

[259] Joel and Michelle Levey.

[260] Roger Walsh, 3.

[261] This framing is based on the work of Robert Hall.

[262] Stan Grof, *The Ultimate Journey: Consciousness and the Mystery of Death*, 317.

BIBLIOGRAPHY

BOOKS

Abdullah, Sharif. *Creating a World that Works for All* (Berrett-Koehler, 1999).

Adams, Douglass. *The Hitchhiker's Guide to the Galaxy* (New York: Ballantine, 1980).

Adams, John. (Ed.) *Transforming Work* (Alexandria: Miles River Press, 1984).

Albrecht, Karl and Ron Zemke. *Service America!* (Homewood: Dow Jones-Irwin, 1985).

Andreas, Connirae. *Core Transformation: Reaching the Wellspring Within* (Moab: Real People Press, 1994).

Ardagh, Arjuna Nick. *Relaxing Into Clear Seeing* (Nevada City: SelfXPress, 1999).

Arrien, Angeles. *The Four-Fold Way* (SanFrancisco: Harper Collins, 1993).

Bennis, Warren and Nanus, Burt. *Leaders* (New York: Harper & Row, 1985).

Blanchard, Kenneth and Peale, Norman Vincent. *The Power of Ethical Management* (New York: William Morow and Company, 1989).

Block, Peter. *The Empowered Manager* (SanFrancisco: Jossey-Bass, 1987).

— *Stewardship* (Berrett-Koehler Publishers, 1993).

Bois, J. Samuel. *The Art of Awareness*, 3rd edition (Dubuque: William C. Brown, 1978).

Bowers, David G. *Systems of Organization* Ann Arbor: University of Michigan Press, 1977)

Brown, Juanita and Isaacs, David. *The World Café*.

Capra, Fritjof. *The Turning Point* (New York: Bantam Books, 1983).

Carey, Ken. *Return of the Bird Tribes* (Kansas City: Uni-Sun, 1988).

Covey, Stephen. *The 7 Habits of Highly Effective People* (New York: Simon & Schuster, 1989).

Dass, Ram. *The Only Dance There Is* (Anchor Books, Garden City, 1974).

Dass, Ram and Paul Gorman. *How Can I Help?* (New York: Alfred A Knop, 1987).

Drucker, Peter. *Management: Tasks, Responsibilities, Practices* (New York: Harper & Row, 1986).

Elgin, Duane. *Voluntary Simplicity* (New York: William Morrow, 1993).

Elkington, John. *Cannibals with Forks* (New Society Publishers, 1998).

Fields, Rick with Peggy Taylor, Rex Weyler, and Rick Ingrasci. *Chop Wood, Carry Water* (Los Angeles: Jeremy P. Tarcher, 1984).

Foley, John. *Driving Out Fear* (Los Alamos Ethics Training and Consulting, 1996).

Fromm, Erich. *To Have Or To Be?* (New York: Harper & Row, 1976).

Gailbraith, Jay. *Organization Design* (Reading: Addison-Wesley, 1977).

Glasser, William. *The Control Theory Manager* (New York: Harper Business, 1994).

Greenleaf, Robert K. *The Servant as Leader* (Robert K. Greenleaf Center, 1970).

— *The Insitution as Servant* (Robet K. Greenleaf Center, 1972).

Grof, Stanislav. *The Adventure of Self-Discovery* (State University of New York Press, 1988).

— *When the Impossible Happens: Adventures in Non-Ordinary Realities.* (Boulder: Sounds True, 2006)
— *The Ultimate Journey: Consciousness and the Mystery of Death* (Ben Lomond: Multidisciplinary Association for Psychedelic Studies, 2006).

Havel, Vaclev. *Summer Meditations* (New York: Alfred A. Knopf, 1992).

Hawley, Jack. *Reawakening the Spirit in Work: The Power of Dharmic Management* (Berrett-Koehler, 1993).

Heider, John. *The Tao of Leadership* (Atlanta: Humanics New Age, 1985).

Jampolsky, Gerald. *Love Is Letting Go of Fear* (Berkeley: Celestial Arts, 1979.

Katie, Byron. *Loving What Is* (New York: Harmony Books, 2002).

Katzenbach, Jon R. and Smith, Douglas K. *The Wisdom of Teams* (New York: Harper Business, 1994).

Kelly, Robert. *The Power of Followership* (New York: Doubleday, 1991).

King, Serge Kahli. *Urban Shaman* (New York: Fireside,1990).

Lao-Tsu. *Tao Te Ching*, translated by Gia-Fu Feng and Jane English (New York: Random House, 1972).

Laszlo, Ervin, *You Can Change the World* (New York: Select Books, 2003).

— *Science and the Akashic Field* (Rochester: Inner Traditions, 2004).

Lawler III, Edward E. *High Involvement Management* (San Francisco: Jossey-Bass, 1987).

Leonard, George. *Adventures in Monogamy* (Los Angeles: Jeremy P. Tarcher).

Levey, Joel and Michelle. *The Fine Arts of Relaxation, Concentration, and Meditation* (Somerville: Wisdom Publications, 2003).

Levine, Stephen. *Who Dies?* (New York: Doubleday, 1982).

Levinson, Harry. *The Exceptional Executive* (Cambridge: Harvard University Press, 1968).

Likert, Rensis. *New Patterns of Management* (New York: McGraw-Hill, 1961).

Lobell, John. *The Little Green Book* (Boulder: Shambhala, 1982).

Massie, Joseph. *The Essentials of Management*, 3rd edition (Englewood Cliffs: Prentice Hall, 1979).

Matthiessen, Peter. *The Snow Leopard* (New York: Viking Press, 1978).

McDonough, William and Braungart, Michael. *Cradle to Cradle* (New York: North Point Press, 2002).

McLagan, Patricia and Christo Nel. *The Age of Participation* (San Francisco: Berrett-Koehler, 1995).

Meyers, David. *The Pursuit of Happiness* (New York: Avon, 1992).

Muller, Wayne. *Sabbath* (New York: Bantam Books, 1999).

Nearing, Helen. *Loving and Leaving the Good Life* (Post Mills: Chelsea Green Publishing Company, 1992).

O'Brien, William J. *The Soul of Corporate Leadership* (Waltham: Pegasus Communications, 1998).

O'Donohue, John. *Anam Cara* (Cliff Street Books, 1997).

Oshry, Barry. *Seeing Systems: Unlocking the Mysteries of Organizational life* (San Francisco: Berrett-Koehler, 1995).

O'Toole, James. *Vanguard Management* (New York: Berkley Publishing Group, 1987).

Owen, Harrison. *Open Space Technology* (San Francisco: Berrett-Koehler, 1997).

Peck, M. Scott. *The Road Less Traveled* (New York: Simon & Schuster, 1978).

Schumacher, E. F. *A Guide for the Perplexed* (New York: Harper & Row, 1977).

Senge, Peter. *The Fifth Discipline: The Art and Practice of the Learning Organization* (New York: Doubleday, 1990).

Sennett, Richard. *Authority* (New York: Alfred A. Knopf, 1980).

Simmons, John and William Mares. *Working Together: Employee Participation in Action* (New York: New York University Press, 1985).

Smith, Huston. *The Religions of Man* (New York: Harper & Row, 1965).

Spears, Larry. (Ed.) *Insights on Leadership* (Nw York: John Wiley & Sons, 1998).

Szekely, Edmond. *Creative Work* (Cartago: International Biogenic Society, 1973).

Underwood, Paula. *The Great Hoop of life* (San Anselmo: Tribe of Two Press, 2000).

United Nations. *Universal Declaration of Human Rights*, United Nations General Assembly: 2nd Session, December 10, 1988, Doc. A/811.

University of Michigan Housing Facilities Department, *Facilities Council Handbook* (Ann Arbor: University of Michigan, 2000).

Walsh, Roger. *Essential Sprituality* (New York: John Wiley & Sons, Inc., 1999).

Weisbord, Marvin and Sandra Janoff. *Future Search* (San Francisco: Berrett-Koehler, 1995).

Whitmyer, Claude. (Ed.) *Mindfulness and Meaningful Work: Explorations in Right Livlihoood* (Berkeley: Parallax Press, 1994).

Wilber, Ken. *No Boundary* (Boston: Shambhala, 1985).

—*Sex, Ecology and Spirituality* (Boston: Shambhala, 1995).

—*A Brief History of Everything* (Boston: Shambhala, 1996).

—*A Theory of Everything* (Boston: Shambhala, 2000).

PERIODICALS

Allan, Kathleen E. "Leadership as an Emergent Property of Individual and Group Interactions," *Inner Edge*, October/November 2000.

Bell, Chip and Ron Zemke. "The Performing Art of Service Management" *Management Review*, July 1990.

Bridges, William and Mitchell, Susan, "Leading Transiton: A New Model for Change," *Leader to Leader*, No. 16, Spring 2000.

Business Week, "Want to Boost Productivity? Try Giving Workers a Say," April 17, 1989.

Carr, Clay. "Managing Self-Managed Workers."

—"7 Keys to Successful Change," *Training*, Februay 1994.

Carr, Geoff, "The Proper Study of Mankind," *The Economist*, December 24th 2005-January 6th 2006.

Chittiser, Joan D. "How Shall We Live?" *Spirituality and Health*, December 2003.

Chomsky, Noam. As quoted in interview by Bill Moyers, "Myth in Our Lives," *Utne Reader*, September/October 1988, 92.

Chomsky, Noam. As quoted in "The Chomsky Tapes, I," *Z Magazine*, October 1995.

Ciefuegos, Paul. "On Changing Corporate Charters," *At Work*, September/October 1997.

Cleveland, Harlan. "Control: The Twilight of Hierarchy," *New Management*, 1985.

Drucker, Peter. "The New Society of Organizations," *Harvard Business Review*, September-October 1992.

—"The New Pluralism," *Leader to Leader*, Fall 1999.

Estes, Ralph and Subashini Ganesan. "The Stakeholder Alliance: A New Bottom Line," *Perspectives on Business and Global Change*, Vol. 11 No. 4.

Hawken, Paul. As quoted in *INC.*, April 1992.

Henning, Joel. "I Make Beautiful: On Being Worthy of the Work We Do," *At Work*, November/December 1997.

Hey, Kenneth R., and Peter D. Moore. "What the Caterpillar Doesn't Know," *Perspectives on Business and Global Change*, Vol. 12 No. 4.

Isaacs, William. "Taking Fight: Dialogue, Collective Thinking, and Organizational Learning," *Organizational Dynamics* (American Management Association, 1993).

Jaworksi. Joseph. "Creating the Future," *The New Leaders*, September/October 1996.

Kelly, Marjorie. "Maximizing Shareholders' Returns: A Legitimate Mandate?" *Perspectives on Business and Global Change*, Vol. 14 No. 1 2000.

—"Taming the Demons of Change" *Business Ethics*, July/August 1993.

Kenny, Robert. "Spread Leadership," *Yes! A Journal of Positive Futures*, Fall 1999.

Kent, Keith. "Call to Servant Leadership," *Facilities Manager*, Fall 1995.

Koenig, Peter. "To Be 'Values Driven' Means Escaping the Profitability Trap," *At Work*, July/August 1997.

Korten, David. "The End of Cowboy Capitalism," *At Work*, May/June 1999.

Kouzes, James and Barry Posner. "The Credibility Factor: What Followers Expect from Their Leaders," *Management Review*, January 1990.

Matusak, Larraine R. "Power."

McLagan, Patricia and Christo Nel. "The Shift to Participation," *Perspectives on Business and Global Change*, Vol. 10 No. 1 1996.

Meadows, Donella. "The Question of Leadership," *In Context*, Number 30.

—"What to Do as a Global Citizen," *Co-Op America Quarterly*, Summer 1992.

Mitlo, Cindy. "A Matter of Principles" *Co-op America Quarterly*, Number 30, Spring 1996.

Moore, Thomas."The Soul of Work," *Business Ethics*, March/April 1993.

Naiman, Linda."Creativity and the Meaning of Work," *Perspectives on Business and Global Change*, Vol. 12 No. 1 1998.

Nirenberg, John. "Creating Workplace Communities," *World Business Academy Perspectives*, Vol. 8 No. 1 1994.

Remen, Rachel Naomi. "Helping, Fixing or Serving?" *Shambhala Sun*, September 1999.

Renesch, John. "Legitimacy: The Power We Give Others," *The New Leaders*, January/February 1996.

Rifkin, Jeremy. "Work," *Utne Reader*, May-June 1995.

Shipka, Barbara. "Relieving Spiritual Poverty in Our Organizations," *World Business Academy Perspectives*, Vol. 7, No. 3, 1999.

Spears, Larry. "Ten Characteristics of the Servant-Leader," *Inner Quest*, 1994 #2.

Surowiecki, James. "Overcompensating," *The New Yorker*, February 13 & 20, 2006, 54.

Wheatley, Margaret J. "The New Story Is Ours to Tell," *Perspectives on Business and Global Change*.

SPEECHES AND ADDRESSES

Block, Peter. Keynote address at 1994 International Conference on Servant-Leadership.

The 14th Dalai Lama. As quoted in *The Asian Age,* 1 January 1995.

Havel, Vaclav. Address to U.S. Congress, 1990.

Tosh, John. Address given at American Management Association Conference in Chicago, April 20,1989.

AUDIO LEARNING PROGRAMS

Beck, Don. *Spiral Dynamics Integral* (Boulder: Sounds True, 2006).

READER'S NOTES _____

ABOUT THE AUTHOR

George SanFacon has over four decades of workplace experience, encompassing an unusually wide range of jobs and settings—grocery clerk, factory assembler, painter, maintenance mechanic, custodian, security guard, high school teacher, short-order cook, facilities engineer, energy conservation consultant, operations manager, management consultant, trainer, facilitator and executive coach. For two decades, he served as Director of the Housing Facilities Department at the University of Michigan, where he pioneered implementing a council-of-equals approach to governance and management using consensus decision making. The organization was nationally recognized for its culture, innovation and effectiveness.

George has facilitated seminars, workshops and retreats on service management, self-directed teams, shared governance, energy conservation, organizational development, dialogue, breathwork, meditation, and servant-leadership. In addition to *A Conscious Person's Guide to the Workplace*, his other writings include:

- *Holistic Servant-Leadership*. This essay, co-authored with Larry C. Spears, outlines a multidimensional approach to servant-leadership. (Available free online through The Spears Center for Servant-Leadership at www.spearscenter.org).

- *Shared Management*. An overview of a unique system of participatory governance and management. (Published in *At Work* magazine.)

- *Facilities Council Handbook*. A hands-on guide for managing an enterprise using a council-of-equals approach to governance and consensus decision making.

George presently works as a part-time caretaker and host at a private retreat center in Michigan, and is also active in the environmental movement. He can be contacted online at gasanfan@umich.edu.

CPSIA information can be obtained at www.ICGtesting.com
Printed in the USA

267999BV00004B/17/P